THE POLITICS OF
NAVAL
SUPREMACY

THE WILES LECTURES
GIVEN AT QUEEN'S UNIVERSITY
BELFAST, 1964

THE POLITICS OF
NAVAL
SUPREMACY

STUDIES IN BRITISH MARITIME
ASCENDANCY

BY

GERALD S. GRAHAM

Rhodes Professor of Imperial History
King's College, University of London

CAMBRIDGE
AT THE UNIVERSITY PRESS
1965

CAMBRIDGE UNIVERSITY PRESS
Cambridge, New York, Melbourne, Madrid, Cape Town, Singapore, São Paulo, Delhi

Cambridge University Press
The Edinburgh Building, Cambridge CB2 8RU, UK

Published in the United States of America by Cambridge University Press, New York

www.cambridge.org
Information on this title: www.cambridge.org/9780521051293

First published 1965
This digitally printed version 2008

A catalogue record for this publication is available from the British Library

Library of Congress Catalogue Card Number: 65–21788

ISBN 978-0-521-05129-3 hardback
ISBN 978-0-521-08279-2 paperback

CONTENTS

To
C. M. G.

PREFACE

The old historians wrote on a wide and generous scale, partly perhaps because they lacked our resources and techniques. Historians of the present age have exploited the mountains of new materials, and refined their techniques, but at the cost of breaking up the comfortable unity that history once provided. Microanalysis of a department, a policy or a tribe is usually accepted as scientific research; by contrast, the 'broad sweep' may be regarded as a hazardous and unscientific indulgence in popular generalization. Yet it is the broad treatment that the Wiles Trust enjoins its lecturers to undertake.

Well aware of the risks that follow acceptance of so candid an instruction, I propose to examine the consequences and limitations of British naval supremacy chiefly within the framework of nineteenth-century politics. Admirals with their fleets, wrote Sir John Fortescue, were 'mere weapons wielded in the hands of the statesman'. Certainly naval history, in the complete sense, cannot be divorced from political and diplomatic history; in the nineteenth century, foreign policy and naval strategy were inseparable.

The Indian Ocean claims particular attention simply because the imperial centre of gravity shifted eastward after the Napoleonic Wars, from the West Indies and the Newfoundland fisheries beyond the Atlantic towards India and China. International rivalries in the Pacific obviously deserve more than perfunctory reference, but until the voluminous records have been winnowed I lack the knowledge to attempt an interpretation of events in that vast, intractable expanse.

Apart from minor alterations the lectures have been printed

as delivered, with the exception of a few paragraphs on the Bagdad railway in chapter III, which I have added as a kind of epilogue to the story of the European *Drang nach Osten*. If the footnotes seem unduly elaborate, at least their length and number may be explained by the compulsion of time; much material which I regarded as relevant was driven out of the text owing to the exigencies of the lecture-hour.

I am very grateful to W. N. Medlicott and Sir Llewellyn Woodward whose wisdom, especially within the field of European diplomacy, was so generously and warmly given. My old friend Commander John Owen has once again helped me with his great nautical learning, and saved me from many a solecism. Various colleagues have come to my aid with their specialized knowledge, and I am indebted to J. R. Alden, C. R. Boxer, M. E. Howard, A. N. Ryan and Ch. Verlinden for critical advice on particular points. Traditional practice and personal pride forbid that I should make them responsible for the errors that inevitably reveal themselves after publication. Two members of my seminar, Ian Steele and John Kendle were good enough to help me with the exacting tasks of checking references and reading proofs. To my hosts, the Committee of the Wiles Trust, the Vice-Chancellor, Dr Michael Grant, and the Professor of Modern History, Michael Roberts, at the Queen's University, Belfast, I should like to express my deep thanks for their constant consideration and generous hospitality.

G. S. G.

Lennoxvale, Belfast
23 May 1964

CHAPTER I

THE ATLANTIC

War at sea is still far from being the most important part of a nation's history; but it has had a considerable determining influence on Britain's development and its prosecution has provided a test of national quality. Yet sea power is a condition which is not in evidence except in time of war. Spectacular battles lighten for brief moments the darkness which by its nature shrouds naval strategy; they are dramatic and sometimes crucial in their importance, but judged over a long span of years they may appear among the lesser incidents of a gigantic struggle.

In the eighteenth and nineteenth centuries sea power was probably most influential when it was least conspicuous. Even in time of peace it functioned as a powerful instrument of diplomatic action and compulsion. The unrestricted mobility of ships, the ease with which they could be moved, often in secrecy, from one rendezvous to another, and the far-reaching effects which the mere threat of intervention could induce—even to the point of dissolving hostile coalitions before they had properly crystallized—have more than once demonstrated the disproportionate impact of naval supremacy on events far inland.[1] By the action of warships national security was lost or maintained, colonial empires expanded or dissolved, and the seaborne trade of belligerents or neutrals was accelerated or stopped.

[1] See Herbert Rosinski, 'Mahan and the Present War', *Brassey's Naval Annual* (London, 1941), pp. 3–7.

Yet, the objects and influence of naval strategy cannot always be deduced from the decisions and actions of admirals and captains; national policies based on the use of sea power cannot be inferred from the movements of warships alone. To appreciate the full influence of sea power on the development of the British empire naval history has to be studied from Cabinet offices in Whitehall as well as from the quarter deck. Naval history is a necessary ingredient of political and diplomatic history, and in practice foreign policy and naval strategy are one. Governments have to run wars 'complete'; and in consequence students of naval history must, at the very least, look for a ministerial policy if they are to understand and adequately interpret the preparation for and conduct of war at sea.

This comprehensive approach to the subject is, on the whole, a comparatively recent development. Until the early years of this century naval history was separated from the main stream of history. One explanation of the curious isolation, it has been suggested, was the difficulty of securing access to high-level political and diplomatic discussions and decisions. As a result, the small coterie of specialists dubbed 'naval historians' had to depend on certain exclusive sources such as official proceedings of admirals at sea. Although this defence of naval history in a vacuum is plausible, it is only partly valid. Materials were available in abundance, but the 'naval historian' confined his researches to salt water narrative, because that was the segment of war that interested him, and in which not infrequently he was professionally expert.[1]

---

[1] In company no doubt with many others I would maintain that novels like Captain Marryat's *Peter Simple* provide as true and authoritative pictures of life at sea in war or peace as any historian can provide.

I would emphasize that his contribution was a considerable one; but wash out the causes of war, the financing of war, the diplomatic relationships with allies or incipient allies, and the movements and operations of armies, and you are left with naval history as formerly written. The student of sea power was 'in irons'.

At the same time, as though to offset the limitations of a professional compartment, this quarantining of naval history was accompanied by a flow of philosophical deductions on the meaning of 'Command of the Sea', a 'Fleet in Being' and such tags as 'he that hath command of the sea can take as much of the war as he listeth' or 'he that is master of the sea may be said in some sort to be master of every country'. (Over the years I have used most of them myself.) Many of such philosophical interpretations, in the hands of great men like Corbett, Mahan and Richmond, were useful, but they have had an unfortunate tendency over the past seventy-five years to repeat themselves—or to revolve in rhetorical circles, like Mynheer with the steam-leg, who could never stop himself, and was seen whirling along with astonishing velocity even after he had become a skeleton.

Not that I underestimate the historical importance of 'command of the sea'; it deserves to be rubbed into British history. Without it there would have been no British empire; without it Britain would have had grave difficulty in securing allies and maintaining domestic security—and the one time she had no allies she lost America; without it Britons would have been perpetually confined to these Islands, and I might not have been born a Canadian! Indeed, it was a member of my own college in London who was responsible for first introducing the serious study of naval records, and interpreting them in terms of the influence of naval supremacy on national history. In 1874 John Knox Laughton, who held the Chair of Modern History at King's College between 1885 and 1912, read a paper at the Royal United Service Institution on 'The Scientific Study of Naval History'. This paper was printed in the *Journal* of that Institution, where some time later it was read by an American captain called Alfred Thayer Mahan, who according to his own admission had not hitherto thought much about history.

Laughton's paper had an explosive effect on Mahan's thinking, and the repercussions, it is fair to say, were felt by the whole world. Mahan plunged deeply into the study of history; his authorities were limited as compared with today, and in some instances unreliable, and the wonder is that he built so well on foundations so inadequate. But the ultimate result was the appearance in 1891 of *The Influence of Sea Power upon History*. No one would suggest that Captain Mahan either discovered, or ever claimed to have discovered, the doctrine of sea power; his own works show how well it was understood by the elder Pitt, and by certain members of the Admiralty during the Napoleonic wars. During the nineteenth century, however, an understanding of the meaning of 'command of the sea' was the privilege of the very few statesmen and seamen who survived those wars; and when they died there were no historians to carry the lessons forward. Probably the greatest historian so far produced by North America is Francis Parkman; yet you have only to compare his two volumes *Montcalm and Wolfe* with Julian Corbett's *England in the Seven Years' War* to recognize that the former was written before, and the latter after Mahan had written *The Influence of Sea Power on History*.

4

But this was no 'conceptual' history, no unsustained theoretical formulation, no parade of ideas unaccompanied by marshalled evidence. Much of the strength of the narrative lies in flat statements which the author attempted to justify on the basis of experience and cogent analysis. Trained in the age of sail, and possessing technical mastery of the tactics of battle and the strategy of naval warfare, he rediscovered and reinterpreted the great traditions of the sailing ship era. On the evidence of a far-flung miscellany of sources, he developed the doctrine of 'command of the sea' and the strategic consequences that followed from it— the effects of 'command' upon land warfare, on the history of west European expansion and on the acquisition and retention of empires. On the basis of centuries of history, he formulated doctrines that were grasped and recklessly applied by Wilhelm II of Germany. I recall Sir Charles Webster's extemporaneous remark in the course of a lecture many years ago: 'Mahan was one of the causes of World War I.'

As a great historical synthesis *The Influence of Sea Power* was a masterpiece, and it remains a classic, but in terms of scholarship it was undoubtedly premature.[1] Because Mahan tended to concentrate on strategy divorced from politics and diplomacy he unwittingly encouraged the quarantining of naval history from the main stream of knowledge. On the other hand, if, as a serving officer, he had managed to find the time to soak himself in the available British documents— the Admiralty IN and OUT letters, Admiralty Instructions, the miscellaneous minutes—do no more than sample the Captains' Logs which represent the diaries of every ship in

---

[1] See Julian Corbett, 'The Revival of Naval History', being the Laughton Memorial Lecture delivered at King's College, London, on 4 October 1916.

commission, and had then delved into the political, economic and diplomatic background of his period, he might well have written only one book; indeed he could hardly have finished *The Influence of Sea Power* on such a scale, and we might have lost the authority and perspective which his peculiar genius for generalization brought to bear on broad strategical problems.

To bring naval history back within the main stream of history required time and toil as well as broad learning. Laughton himself prepared the way when he founded the Navy Records Society for the systematic collection and interpretation of relevant documents. The present series—105 volumes up to date—show the interconnection between politics, commerce, finance and naval strategy, and demonstrate conclusively the senselessness of trying to isolate one kind of knowledge in a compartment. But it is a far call from a hundred or so printed volumes of documents and an acre of Foreign and Colonial Office papers, to a new integration of naval and British history; and there is an abysmal gulf between saying what should be done, and the doing of it. The easiest, and not the least impressive inaugural lecture is the kind that describes with scholarly acumen what the other fellow should do.

Although fully aware of the weakness of this cowardly approach, I am tempted to point out that while problems of naval strategy demand relevant knowledge of foreign policy, naval projects and operations badly need investigation from a united service point of view—in relation to the land as well as the sea. One must not push the national importance of sea power too far; it would be an historical error to attempt to shove heroes like Clive or Wolfe, Marlborough or Wellington too far into the shade of the admirals. British governments have rarely been unaware of the need for a strong naval force. They have been more often guilty of neglecting to maintain an army capable of providing a home defence force, and, even more important, a field force for European or overseas operations, or for what I like to call Foreign Office or Colonial Office wars.

In the great wars of the eighteenth century and even in the twentieth, Britain was usually supported by allies on the European continent; these allies wanted primarily front-line troops because they were concerned with the elimination of the enemy as an active opponent *on land*. To put the army in Europe, or overseas, naturally required command of the sea, and occasionally the struggle between whale and elephant produced an equilibrium that could only be broken on land. Nelson's decisive battles of the Nile and Trafalgar, which led to the downfall of French sea power, were followed by Napoleon's destruction of the continental armies at Austerlitz, Jena and Wagram. The Battle of the Nations near Leipzig in October 1813 was the decisive battle for the liberation and reclamation of Europe.[1] Final possession of European territory was the consequence of victory on land—the demolition of Napoleon's army.

It is well to remember too that as long as an enemy could win victories on land, in Europe or overseas, he could always enter the market of peace negotiations with valuable bargaining counters. What was lost by defeat at sea might be retrieved at the peace table. During the Seven Years War in

[1] The Nile was fought on 1 August 1798; Trafalgar on 21 October 1805; Austerlitz on 2 December 1805; Jena on 14 October 1806; Wagram on 5–6 July 1809; Leipzig on 16–19 October 1813. A special medal was struck for Waterloo, but not for Trafalgar.

India, the French held local mastery of the sea for a considerable time, but were beaten on land; and with the defeat of their army they lost the struggle in India, because their victories at sea gave them no bargaining advantages at the peace. British ministers were very much aware of this constant factor in peace negotiations; it was not only the needs of home security that prompted Britain to support costly expeditionary forces and prickly allies; they had to do it to make sure of winning the war, and for that purpose an effective army was essential.

In short, warfare has been and remains ultimately based on land, and primarily directed against an enemy's land forces. At sea there is no defined territory which a naval squadron can occupy, and on which its commanders can assert an enduring authority. The sea is a passive, unlimited, empty medium except to the fisherman. To the trader, it provides only a route, and in essence, command of the sea means little more than the control of shipping passing along such routes. 'The importance which attaches to the command of the sea', read an Admiralty memorandum of 1902, 'lies in the control which it gives over sea communications. The weaker sea-power is absolutely unable to carry to success any large military expedition over sea....'[1] In other words, naval warfare is concerned with the maintenance of maritime communications through the destruction of the enemy's power

[1] Memorandum on Imperial Defence presented to the Colonial Conference of 1902 (A. Berriedale Keith (ed.), *Selected Speeches and Documents on British Colonial Policy, 1763–1917* (Oxford, 1933), II, 230). 'Keeping of the sea routes inviolate' became an Admiralty dogma of the nineteenth century. In the opinion of Lt.-Cmdr. D. W. Waters, R.N., such an emphasis on communications, by encouraging a strategy of blockade and patrol, led to a neglect of shipping *per se*, and was responsible for the disastrous Admiralty failure to organize a convoy system at the beginning of World War I.

to break them, and not, as in land warfare, with the conquest of territory.[1] By winning control of the main traffic lines, not only was the superior navy in a position to exert pressure on the enemy shore; it could and did prevent that enemy from using the bulk of his shipping for his own commercial or military benefit. Success in this endeavour did not necessarily mean the end of the conflict, but it contributed to the ultimate strategic objective: the complete reduction of the enemy's strength.

Thanks to the immunity from interference provided by this control a small country like Britain could exercise a world weight far beyond her resources in manpower and wealth. With superior strength at sea she could obtain swift and far-reaching results by isolated victories. However indeterminate its effects on the balance of power on the Continent, sea power was likely to be decisive in its results overseas, where the territories in question were dependent for sustenance on the mother country in Europe. As the long maritime struggle with France revealed, the inferior contender was incapable of safeguarding distant colonies. Because of its indivisibility—'the sea is one' was an old Admiralty maxim—the control of the oceans was bound to go to the superior belligerent, who by cutting his opponent's communications could mop up his colonies at leisure.

In this manner, Britain was able, in the course of three centuries, to win a major share of the non-European spoils that Columbus and Vasco da Gama had first glimpsed from their decks. During this time she was able to eliminate in

---

[1] Corbett, *Principles*, pp. 80–1. In this connection, see Friedrich Ratzel, *Das Meer als Quelle der Völkergrösse, Eine Politisch-Geographische Studie* (Munich and Berlin, 2nd ed. 1911), especially pp. 73–81.

succession her Spanish, Dutch and French rivals for empire; and not until she collided with self-sufficient colonies during the War of American Independence did this almost un-interrupted career of maritime expansion come temporarily to a stop. With its revival during the War of the French Revolution, the almost automatic process of acquisition began again. By 1815 an overseas empire, whose original focus had been the North Atlantic, almost encircled the world—from Canada and the Caribbean in the west around the Cape of Good Hope to India and Australia, and, by the second quarter of the nineteenth century, eastward to the islands of the Pacific. With the 'inevitability of gradualness' the geography of the sea had shaped Britain's destiny. Command of the sea meant a practical monopoly of communications throughout the oceans of the world, including most of the great gateways—the Straits of Dover and the English Channel, the Strait of Gibraltar, the entrance to the Indian Ocean around the Cape, and even before the occupation of Aden and Singapore, the Strait of Bab-el-Mandeb and the Straits of Malacca. In the words of Sir Halford Mackinder: 'When the Napoleonic War was over, British sea-power encompassed, almost without competition, that great world-promontory which stands forward to the Cape of Good Hope from between Britain and Japan.'[1]

In the beginning, however, there was little beyond the occasional plundering raid to suggest the coming struggle for empire. For half a century after the first Columbus expedition, no European state seriously opposed the claims of Spain or Portugal as set down in the Treaty of Tordesillas of 1494. French and English searches for a north-west passage to the

---

[1] *Democratic Ideals and Reality* (Pelican edition, London, 1944), p. 49.

Indies were merely cautious attempts to open up trade routes
well out of range of Spanish armaments in the Caribbean.
Similarly their colonial projects were concerned only with
the outskirts of Spanish or Portuguese territory; the choice of
sites far up the St Lawrence river or on the shores of Newfoundland was deliberate, because both countries were anxious
to avoid military conflict with Spain. England and France, and
subsequently Holland, could do no more than conduct pilot
schemes of empire until they were in a position to defend their
possessions and secure their communication by sea. French-
men and Englishmen might harry the Spaniard or the Portuguese, but to attempt colonization in any but the more remote
and less profitable regions of the earth was to invite disaster.

Yet statesmen in England, as elsewhere, were slow to
grasp the importance of controlling maritime communications in the interests of expanding trade and national
power. It was difficult to understand that in contrast to
warfare on land, superiority at sea could mean, not only the
conclusive elimination of an enemy, but a practical monopoly
of ocean communications. Moreover, until Hawkins set
down in impressive memorials the strategic advantages of
isolating Spain from her empire, few Englishmen, if any,
believed that the cutting of Spanish sea communications
could reduce the military capacity of a great European state.
The expeditions of the early Elizabethan sea-dogs were semi-
piratical raids, wherein hopes of immediate profit and hatred
of popery counted for far more than any strategical design,
such as that of defeating Spain by eliminating her *flotas*. There
was no conviction that the ship might be a decisive instrument of national power, or that naval warfare might appreci-
ably affect the result of any European struggle on land.

Nevertheless, national interest was beginning to invade the Atlantic jousting lists. By the eighties, the apparently haphazard character of English raids on Spanish commerce seemed to strike a pattern; after 1585 plans were projected for attacking not only Spanish coastal harbours, but such strategic areas as San Domingo, Cartagena and Panama. There were discussions, too, on the possible occupation of Havana and the blockade of Mexican ports. These were more than mere schemes of pillage; they involved an organized offensive against the Spanish colonial empire as the source of Spanish economic power. For example, Drake's onslaughts of 1585–6 helped to paralyse Philip's campaign in Flanders by depriving Parma of the money to keep up the army. In 1590, when Frobisher and Hawkins waylaid the annual *flota*, Spain had to forgo her anticipated invasion of France. Even the plundering of Spanish coastal harbours, when viewed in retrospect, seems to be something more than a beard-singeing diversion. 'The truth is', wrote the Venetian ambassador in 1587, 'that he [Drake] has done so much damage on these coasts of Spain alone, that though the King were to obtain a signal victory against him he would not recover one half the loss he has suffered.'[1]

The first evidence of a groping towards some tactical scheme for sailing ships revealed itself in the battle with the Spanish Armada—the first major artillery duel at sea. The Spaniards carried a preponderance of heavy pieces sufficient to smash the English fleet, at close quarters, but the English wisely refused to come within range. Their own light-shotted, longer-ranged guns were not powerful enough to do

[1] J. S. Corbett, *Papers Relating to the Navy during the Spanish War, 1585–87* (Navy Record Society, no. XI, 1898), p. xliii.

serious execution at so great a distance. Yet, it can be said that English seamen by 1588 had learned the value of the ship, not merely as a vehicle for carrying men, but as an instrument of seamanship and gunnery designed to fight other ships with tactical advantage.[1]

Although naval warfare remained for many years a highly individualistic procedure, the defeat of the Spanish forces pointed the way to future state-organized fleets manned and directed by professional fighting seamen. Already the warship was ceasing to be regarded as a mere transport for troops engaged, like the Armada, to cover a land invasion. In the approaching era of established navies, the line-of-battle ship was to become accepted as an exclusively fighting vessel. Squadrons of warships, divided into rates according to the number of guns they carried, took the place of the improvised fleets of Elizabeth's time, and professional seamen were soon wrestling with the problem of deploying large numbers of ships to achieve concentration and thus utilize the full force of their fire power. The separation of the man-of-war from the mass of merchantmen was not, however, completed until nearly the end of the seventeenth century. In an emergency, the established squadrons had to be supplemented by merchantmen which, although gradually differentiated from warships, continued for some time to be little inferior in fighting capacity. During the battles with the Dutch in 1665, the proportion of merchantmen engaged was nearly one in four.[2]

[1] See Michael Lewis, *Armada Guns: A Comparative Study of English and Spanish Armaments* (London, 1961).

[2] The chief limitations affecting the performance of the early navies were supply and health. It was impossible to provide sufficient stores or to keep men fit for more than a few weeks at a time. Not until the end of the eighteenth century could large ships remain at sea for prolonged periods.

A new element—hardly perceptible at first—had thus been thrown into the scales of the European balance—sea power. In the past, territorial expansion, founded on military land force, had been the principal issue of European rivalry. With the seventeenth century, competition for empire on the oceans very gradually superimposed itself on the traditional pattern of continental relationships. It was obvious that the riches of the New World as well as of Asia were available only to those nations which possessed sufficient fleets to acquire and then transfer them.

As a consequence of this centrifugal pull from the oceans, European national interests tended to develop a certain dualism. Imperial policies that were concerned with sea routes and colonies began to conflict with policies of continental expansion. Yet even where continental ambition finally prevailed, as in the case of France, every European state with a frontage on the Atlantic had, at least, to revise its calculations on the essential components of state policy. The English Channel had taken the place of the cloistered Mediterranean as the main field of conflict, because the Atlantic powers were best situated in terms of geography as well as skills and capital to carry out the exploitation of the New World.

Up to about the mid-seventeenth century, English and Dutch stood generally together against Spain. Although sometimes hostile to each other in the Indian Ocean there was a kind of tacit understanding that they should not quarrel over colonial interests in North America. Even after the execution of Charles I, the 'understanding' held good for a time; competing boundaries on the American coastline were ignored. Indeed, apart from a small isolated post on the

Hudson river the Dutch left the North American continent alone—preferring to concentrate in the East Indies. Similarly Dutch and English islands in the West Indies were unaffected by the growing commercial rivalry, although both countries were alert to possible Spanish interventions. But when Spain ceased to count, gradually the latent fears and suspicions of expanding competitors came to the surface, and commercial rivalry became the basic cause of a series of violent wars spread over some twenty years—a bloody interval that makes the second half of the seventeenth century one of the decisive periods in English imperial history.

During this time Englishmen began to grasp the fundamental principle of 'command of the sea'. The statesmen of Cromwell's Commonwealth and especially Blake, were the first to appreciate its implications, namely, that only constant supremacy at sea offered any hope of achieving simultaneously the defence of the English coast and the far-flung trade routes that led to an expanding colonial empire. The only effective security was to destroy the enemy's main forces in battle, or hold him in harbour by means of blockade. There was no limited alternative as in land warfare, because there were no fortresses, entrenchments or natural obstacles like mountains and rivers to induce a protective stalemate or equilibrium. By the end of the first Dutch war, and, for the first time in English history, the complete elimination of the enemy became an accepted strategic objective.

Under Cromwell too the needs of trade began to dictate the long-term objectives of the English colonial policy. They were responsible for the establishment of a uniform system of trade regulations, expressed in a growing body of navigation laws. The earlier navigation laws were not intended to be measures of military security; in practice, however, despite the lack of proper enforcement machinery, they evolved as such. By forbidding the carriage of English goods in ships other than English, and by confining the imports of Asia, Africa and America to English ships, they encouraged the growth of an English mercantile marine at the expense of Britain's rivals.

By the second half of the seventeenth century, then, we are at the beginning of a new age. After 1660—following the long period of internal disruption and civil war—the commercial empire of England began to take recognizable shape. In 1694 Lord Halifax paid tribute to the navy that defended and extended trade as 'the life and soul of government'; but he might, with a little more prescience, have drawn attention to the new instruments of finance—the Bank of England founded in that same year, and the national debt established in the previous year—which, along with the new Board of Trade and Plantations, were to occupy an equally central and influential place in government.

There was now a growing disposition to identify overseas commerce with military strength, and, because colonies counted simply as commerce, there was no demand for territorial conquest. British governments were not interested in sending armies to extend Anglo-Saxon dominion overseas. Canada, for example, might have been taken almost any time after 1692 had there been the will. According to good mercantilist logic, colonial commerce could be most cheaply secured by means of outposts or factories, supplied and defended by ships of war; protection of colonial trade need *not* include the defence of burdensome territorial pickings across the oceans. A growing network of overseas bases could provide essential local protection; the decisive action— the destruction of the main enemy fleet—could be achieved in or about home waters.[1]

It was not until William Pitt came to power that the conquest of overseas territories became an avowed object of British strategy. Yet this change must not be interpreted as marking any profound alteration in British policy. Pitt's assault on French possessions was founded partly on a desire to safeguard the Thirteen Colonies in North America by conquering Canada, and chiefly on an almost fanatical urge to weaken France in Europe. By totally eliminating the French empire, Pitt intended to safeguard the traditional European balance of power, or, more accurately, tilt it in England's favour. He was convinced that the destruction of French commerce was the key to Britain's home security. He believed—and the significant thing is that other great exponents of sea power and colonial expansion, like the Duc de Choiseul, also believed—that colonial trade and the sources of colonial trade were no longer simply important accessories of strength, but elements of *decisive* weight on the scales of the European balance. 'Upon the navy', wrote Choiseul, 'depend the colonies, upon the colonies commerce, upon commerce the capacity of a state to maintain numerous armies, to increase its population and to make possible the most glorious and most useful enterprises.' The French Foreign Minister had learned his lesson from Pitt.

---

[1] The function of bases was not dissimilar to that of convoy escorts; they were designed to insure particular trades or trading areas against guerrilla attacks, or roving expeditions that might perchance break through the British coastal blockade; their existence was fundamental to the exercise of British power and influence overseas.

This intensification of British interest in colonial trade expansion was not, of course, a sudden development. At the beginning of the eighteenth century the propaganda of trading and financial interests was already promoting the conviction that maritime commerce and naval power were indissoluble. Naval wars were beginning to affect directly the interests of large numbers of business men. The War of the Spanish Succession had been the first essentially 'business man's war', waged quite as much to determine who should possess the Spanish colonial trade, as who should possess the Spanish crown. The sequence had been a 'business man's peace', which made provision for Britain's commercial expansion overseas. Thenceforward, the trading, shipbuilding and financial interests, on whose support the Hanoverian dynasty relied so heavily, considered naval subsidies as necessary business insurance. The records of the Board of Trade are enough to show the ubiquitous activity and mounting influence on government of highly organized business groups. These groups were continually lobbying for special protection, and not infrequently were responsible for the deflection of naval strength in the interest of local defence. The British 'cruiser acts' of the early eighteenth century were largely a consequence of their self-centred persistence. 'Of the great part of the regulations concerning the colony trade,' wrote Adam Smith, 'the merchants who carry it on, it must be observed, have been the principal advisers.'

Indeed, the British mercantile community was beginning to look upon war as an exceedingly profitable undertaking. During the War of the Spanish Succession, French and Spanish commerce had been swept from the seas, and, equally significant from the merchants' point of view, Dutch competition had been drastically weakened. Holland had been almost destroyed by the very wars which, in alliance with Britain, she had so actively helped to win.

It is understandable, therefore, that twenty-five years after the Treaty of Utrecht, merchants formed the vanguard of citizen patriots who almost hysterically demanded the complete breaking of the Spanish colonial monopoly in revenge for Captain Jenkins' missing ear. In the opinion of the city the capture of each French or Spanish island represented a double gain, since the resulting increase of English trade was accompanied by a proportionate weakening of French trade. There was a certain basis of logic in this reasoning. The sole object of any war on commerce is to carry on campaigns at sea with such intensity that they will ultimately lead to the starvation of the enemy in terms of raw materials and finance. By cutting the flow of produce and specie from French and Spanish overseas colonies, Britain was able to make a dent on the military power of their respective mother countries, while the additional wealth diverted to her own coffers did make it easier for her to subsidize allies on the continent of Europe.

On the other hand, there is no evidence to suggest that the denial of colonial commerce materially altered the French strategic position on the Continent, and it was with France as chief rival that Britain was principally concerned. Loss of 'command of the sea' diminished but never dangerously reduced French resources and staying-power. There was not, as many historians in the past have tended to believe, a 'strangulation' of France by English sea power during the two wars between 1744 and 1762, because overseas trade was *not* the backbone of French national strength. The fact that a high total of French shipping was destroyed, or that a large part of the French mercantile marine was unable to leave harbour as a result of a British blockade means little, unless the total of overseas trade is measured against the national economy as a whole. Admittedly, the French colonial trade was an extremely valuable war asset, but recent investigations would suggest that it was a useful buttress rather than a foundation. The Seven Years War served to demonstrate that France could live for a prolonged period without colonial trade, and still fight a war effectively.

The strength of France lay neither in precarious alliances nor tenuous connections overseas, but in the indigenous resources of land, and more especially of population, which enabled her to recuperate with astonishing speed after a disastrous war, to re-equip a powerful army and to maintain it for prolonged periods. At the beginning of the eighteenth century, her population was about sixteen millions, as compared with England's six, and Holland's two and a half millions. The wars of Louis XIV had left her exhausted, but territorially she had suffered little damage. With a far larger area than Britain, France also possessed a proportionately larger percentage of arable land, which meant that she could feed a proportionately more numerous population from her own resources than could Britain.[1] She was, in short, almost self-sufficient.

It should be remembered, however, that France was in many respects an amphibious state. The long coastline bordering on the two great seas, the Atlantic and the Mediterranean, not only bred a race of superb seamen, but inevitably

[1] Arthur L. Dunham, *The Industrial Revolution in France 1815–1848* (New York, 1955), p. 420.

stimulated the maritime and commercial ardour of French governments. Providence, Richelieu had once remarked, offered France the 'empire of the seas' by generously providing harbours on two coasts; and certainly French history has demonstrated that she remained sufficiently maritime to be continuously attracted by the prospects of expansion overseas. And yet this great maritime inheritance, and the huge resources of a rich land and of a versatile people (who seemed to possess a special aptitude for colonization), were not sufficient to provide for a durable overseas empire. At a time when France was the strongest and the wealthiest of the great powers of Europe she forged no enduring political ties either in Canada, Louisiana, India or in any other of her distant insular possessions. Although she built fine fleets and trained fine seamen, their achievement was, on the whole, ephemeral.

Was this failure owing to any 'natural aptitude' on the part of the English who defeated them? In terms of geography could France be considered less of a 'natural sea power' than Britain? One may perhaps define a 'natural sea power' as a state whose security and very existence is rooted in the sea. But this condition was not entirely true of England until her empire had been fairly established and had become an asset to her national economy. The English people at the beginning of their imperial career had no great tradition of the sea to compare, say, with that of the Scandinavians or the Arabs. There was no instinctive compulsion to 'rule the waves'. Before the sixteenth century, England had been an agricultural country, continental in her outlook rather than maritime and expansionist. Until Elizabeth's reign interest remained chiefly landward. It was the acquisition and consolidation of an empire that imposed during the next two centuries the development of a navy sufficiently strong to safeguard, against at least two European powers, the mother country and her overseas possessions.

Such an argument may suggest that sea power is essentially an artificial creation, dependent on the whims and policies of kings and parliaments, and to a considerable extent this is true.[1] On the other hand, it is probably fair to say that steady political concentration on maritime affairs was only possible in an insular state. British governments showed greater consistency in the building and maintenance of fleets which alone could secure an overseas empire, simply because they were not handicapped, as were the French, by the conflicting interests of two frontiers, land and sea. 'An insular state', wrote Mahan, cryptically if somewhat turgidly,' ...contemplates wars from a position of antecedent probable superiority from the two-fold concentration of its policy; defence and offense being closely identified, and energy, if exerted judiciously, being fixed upon the increase of naval force to the clear subordination of that more narrowly styled military.'[2]

Unlike continental countries such as France or Holland, Britain, because of the English Channel, could afford to neglect her army and still remain a first-class power. Or—to put it another way—since the development of a predominant naval force made it economically impracticable to maintain

[1] Why the Chinese never developed sea power is still a much-debated question. They had the resources and the skills to do so had their rulers wished, and if they had created sea-going fleets, which was within their power to do, North America might have become even before the days of Columbus an Oriental and not an Anglo-Saxon appanage. For a discussion of this problem, see G. B. Sansom, *The Western World and Japan* (London, 1950), pp. 42–5, 47, 147–8.

[2] *Retrospect and Prospect* (London, 1902), pp. 163–4.

a British army of continental proportions, security against invasion depended upon the fleet; and as long as a strong fleet was maintained in home water, the soil of Britain was rarely in danger. Command of the Narrow Seas—the North Sea, the Western Mediterranean, the English Channel and the Bay of Biscay—enabled Britain to watch, control and often demolish the main naval forces of Spain, Holland or France. From home ports, or from advanced bases on the fringe of Europe, like Gibraltar or Port Mahon, Britain could in a sense isolate Europe, and yet, almost automatically, maintain naval superiority in all the seas of the world. On occasion when enemy fleets succeeded in evading the west European cordon, they were chased overseas, as was Villeneuve by Nelson. In other words, from home bases which proved to be immune from invasion, Britain was able not only to conduct distractionary raids and support limited campaigns, but also, as I have mentioned, to cut the flow of enemy bullion and other economic necessities from overseas sources.

Admittedly the exigencies of domestic politics frequently intruded to the detriment of English imperial objectives. The development of a navy, for instance, was seriously affected by the failure of Charles I to convince his subjects that 'ship-money' was more than a shabby political manœuvre. During the War of the Spanish Succession the struggle between Tories and Whigs became in part a struggle between the maritime and continental interests of the nation. The Jacobites of Hanoverian times, and sometimes the Cobdenites of Victorian, had to be considered before governments could take decisive action in matters of imperial security.

But these conflicts of interest in England were merely

episodic; they were not, as in France, chronic. France could not escape the political dilemma which confronted every continental power with a frontage on the Atlantic. Geography, national interest and trade demanded of the French both a first-class army and a strong navy. Overseas trade helped to support an army, but there was less and less to share with the navy. In an era of increased trade competition, recurrent dynastic wars and larger professional armies, the financial pressures sustained by incompetent governments were enormous. France wanted continental power and security, and she wanted an overseas empire, but even her great resources were not sufficient to bear the crushing weight of military charges that were necessary to achieve both. Maritime effort became, therefore, a matter of intermittent enthusiasms; and in comparison with continental considerations, the business of empire in the eighteenth century never amounted to much more than an important French side-line. Hence it is not surprising that both the Seven Years War and the Napoleonic Wars were, as contests for overseas colonies, very one-sided struggles. With the exception of the War of American Independence, when a continental coalition gave her temporary superiority, France had to count on losing the war at sea.

The American Revolution began as a mere civil rebellion and developed into what we might call a Colonial Office war; then, when European nations began to participate, it became a full-scale Foreign Office war. Mr Mackesy's notable contribution to grand strategy has provided a long-needed trans-oceanic perspective.[1] British policy and performance

[1] Piers Mackesy, *The War for America, 1775–1783* (London, 1964).

can only be fully intelligible when examined in the light of continental strategy *vis-à-vis* a world-wide maritime strategy that was further complicated by the novel perplexities of civil conflict.

In the beginning, the war might conceivably have remained localized, but whether the colonies could have been subdued in isolation is another question. True, Britain would have been free to transport across the Atlantic the necessary supplies and armies without interference; communications with the British bases in America would have been secure. None the less, victory could only have been won by the destruction of the American armed forces, in a vast land that had attained something like self-sufficiency. As it happened, the action of France turned a local colonial struggle into a world war. The purely naval operations of this war have been described by Mahan, and his scholarly successors in the United States have knitted these events to the involved political and military strategies of the times.[1] The story usually ends with the indeterminate action of Chesapeake Bay that led to the surrender of General Cornwallis on 19 October 1781 and the final recognition of the Thirteen Colonies as an independent nation. Consequently, we have the traditional assumption that victory was the consequence of French naval intervention.

In one sense, of course, the argument is undeniable, since the temporary command of the sea achieved by the combined French-Spanish forces in the American and West Indies theatre was decisive. Chesapeake Bay was a trifling engagement as battles go; yet it did seal independence because it prevented the relief of Cornwallis's army, and led to its sur-

[1] See, for example, John R. Alden, *The American Revolution* (New York, 1954).

25

render at Yorktown. On the other hand to suggest that *only* French intervention in North American waters could have won independence for the United States is an oversimplification. Even if there had been no Yorktown—even if Britain had not temporarily lost command of the sea—it is unlikely that the mother country could have quelled the rebellion, and won the war. As long as British troops were regularly supplied from home, they might well have kept their footholds in New York or Charleston; but the occupation of a few scattered coastal segments did not necessarily mean the subjugation of a vast area that was largely in a position to support its own forces. Since the American colonies were self-sufficient in food supplies, and only in small part dependent on Europe for munitions and money, a successful blockade of the French and Spanish ports would not have ended the struggle. The decision had to be achieved on the continent of North America. But British resources had already been stretched too thinly to meet the strategic commitments of a two-hemisphere war.[1] Bereft of allies, and occupied with three considerable European enemies, Britain could hardly have found the resources and the men to subdue a bristling quarter of a continent, three thousand miles away. Supremacy at sea would not alone have given Britain the upper hand on land.[2]

Chesapeake Bay signalized the downfall of the first British empire, but the importance of this curious engagement in the history of British naval strategy is equally significant. Chesapeake Bay demonstrated beyond all doubt that British 'command of the sea' was a precarious monopoly

[1] Cf. Mackesy, *op. cit.* pp. 367, 512–13.
[2] G. S. Graham, *Empire of the North Atlantic* (2nd ed. London, 1958), pp. 215–16.

and a deceptive concept unless buttressed by effective alliances on the Continent. Neither administrative weakness, nor military and naval ineptitude was responsible for the humiliating disaster. The dominating factor was political isolation.

In other words, without allied reinforcements to divert or pin down enemy forces, the Royal Navy was not, and never has been, strong enough to ensure ultimate victory in a major conflict. Twenty years later, despite control of the Mediterranean as well as the Atlantic, Britain had to make peace on Napoleon's terms after the defeat of the Second Coalition. Naval supremacy could not of itself bring about a decision. On the other hand, possession of this unique power proved to be the warranty of ultimate victory; it enabled Britain to intervene repeatedly and influentially on the continent of Europe. Diversionary actions such as surprise landings, the cutting of coastal supply lines, the convoying of reinforcements and supplies, the occupation of off-shore islands—indeed, substantial campaigns, whether in Spain or in distant theatres from the Cape and Mauritius to Java and the Spice Islands—helped to distract Napoleon and sap the military strength of France. By such means, Britain was able to attract and resuscitate allies and to rebuild the overwhelming coalition which moved relentlessly to the final decision at Waterloo.

During the next hundred years, as the Industrial Revolution gained momentum, the direct impact of technology on weapons, supply and transport, gradually made itself felt in the military field. Both the railway and the telegraph promoted the mobility of land warfare—encouraging the swift campaigns of movement which Napoleon had inaugurated.[1] Yet naval strategy barely moved beyond the point it had reached by the end of the eighteenth century. As late as 1911, Admiral Mahan, in his introduction to *Naval Strategy*, could see no technological developments that seriously affected the concept of naval warfare as inherited from the sailing ship era.[2] Indeed the coming of the steamship, the submarine cable and the wireless telegraph served to strengthen control of naval operations from the centre, while the growing dependence of the great powers on overseas raw materials enhanced, in the event of a long-drawn war, the efficacy of naval blockade. In Mahan's view, command of the sea was still identical with world power.

With the coming of the submarine and the aeroplane, however, Mahan's doctrine lost its general validity. New instruments—ships that moved under the sea as well as ships that flew above it—were not only threatening the traditional

[1] 'No other development of the Industrial Revolution', wrote Major-General J. F. C. Fuller of the railway, 'had so profound an influence on the future of peace and war' (*The Conduct of War, 1789–1961* (London, 1961), p. 92).

The development of a railway network throughout the Continent helped to redress the balance of land power *vis-à-vis* the sea. British naval interventions in the eighteenth and early nineteenth centuries had been facilitated by superior mobility, which was accelerated with the coming of steam. The unbarricaded sea was ONE. Now the railroad was to offer what the aeroplane was to complete: a command of the land.

The possibility of transporting troops and guns rapidly across country to any threatened point of attack, not only increased continental self-sufficiency, it severely reduced, or at least appeared to reduce, the ability of the leading sea power to intervene effectively as Nelson had intervened in Egypt and Italy, or Wellington in Spain. During the second half of the nineteenth century, astute generals like Moltke felt capable of dealing with any serious landing within twenty-four hours. See Herbert Rosinski, 'Sea Power in Global Warfare of the Future', *Brassey's Naval Annual* (London, 1947), p. 106; also, by same author, 'The Evolution of the Conduct of War and of Strategic Thinking', *U.S. Naval War College, Naval Warfare Course* (1956), VI, 13.

[2] (London, 1911), pp. 2–8.

British supremacy; as we shall see in a subsequent lecture, they were about to break the old European pattern of imperialism. Such developments in no way invalidated Mahan's concept of the traditional indivisibility of the oceans. Whatever the rising weight and influence of continental land and air power, the sea was still *one*; but within that medium the traditional two-hemisphere role of the Royal Navy was no longer practicable. The aeroplane was rapidly restoring the world of Ptolemy, a small and shrunken world, not of oceans containing huge island continents, but of great stretches of land divided by gigantic lakes.

In a uniquely prescient lecture to the Royal Geographical Society in 1904, that remarkable man, Sir Halford Mackinder, looking backward to the origins of maritime empire, predicted that the unity of the land was about to become the vital element in what we today call 'global strategy'. He prophesied that the landlocked peoples of eastern Europe, western and central Asia, would establish the 'Eurasian Heartland', eventually moulding Europe, Asia and Africa into a single continent—'the World Island'—immune from, and indisputably master of, the oceans.[1]

This had been the Napoleonic dream, which in the nineteenth century sometimes became the British nightmare—a recurrent nightmare based on the fear that a continental alliance by making itself master of the 'Eurasian Heartland'

---

[1] 'Who rules East Europe commands the Heartland:
Who rules the Heartland commands the World-Island:
Who rules the World-Island commands the World.'

(*Democratic Ideals and Reality* (Pelican ed.), p. 113.)

See also, 'The Geographical Pivot of History', read on 25 January 1904 (*Geographical Journal*, XXIII (1904)). Reprinted in *The Scope and Methods of Geography and the Geographical Pivot of History* (London, 1951), with an introduction by E. W. Gilbert, p. 30.

would not only exclude British trade, but could strike at the peripheral British empire anywhere, from Egypt and the Straits, to India and the Far East. Likewise, it was based on the fear that the application of such a continental system would be combined, in the Napoleonic manner, with the creation of fleets sufficient eventually to overwhelm or reduce by attrition the naval power of Great Britain. As it happened, almost a hundred years elapsed before the apparition materialized, and, in the course of two World Wars, Britain was able to fend off disaster, chiefly as a result of allied naval supremacy. Indeed, sea power made it possible for the Anglo-American powers to intervene directly and decisively on the continent of Europe.[1]

But the days when command of the sea was the prerequisite of victory were already numbered. Technological developments of the past twenty years have finally brought an end to the historic tug-of-war between the elephant and the whale. The kind of equilibrium which permitted the existence of a dominant naval power in the nineteenth century, is no longer practicable. Today, a maritime state can offer no effective counterweight to the consolidated resources and manpower of continental monoliths. Mackinder's concept of an over-all global strategy based on the unity of the land mass remains plausible in terms of the present balance of power; but it must be left to wiser men than myself to forecast whether events now shaping in this nuclear age will produce a world island based on control of the land, a world concert of nations based on deadlock, or no world at all!

[1] Herbert Rosinski, 'Sea Power in Global Warfare of the Future', p. 108.

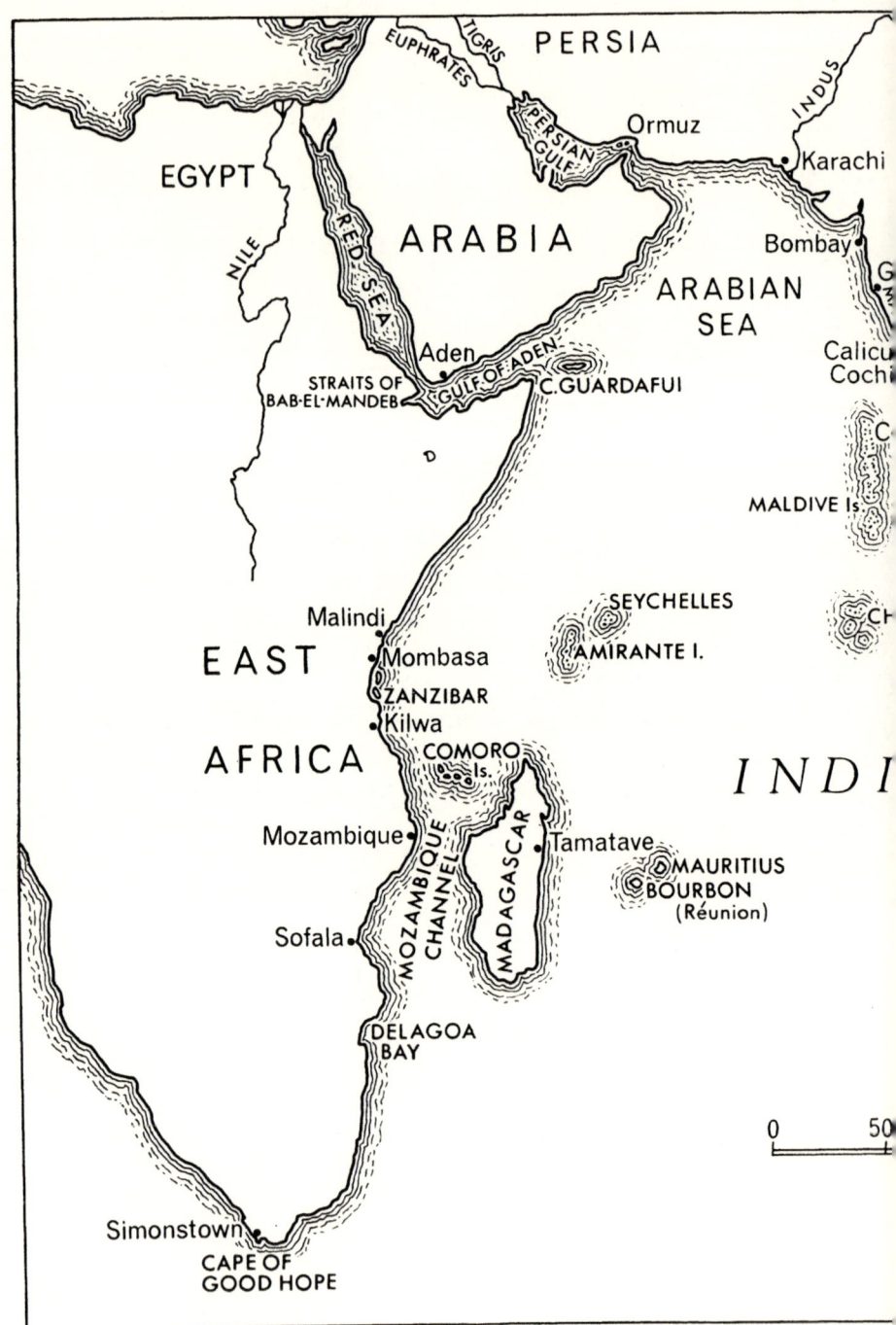

The Indian Ocean:

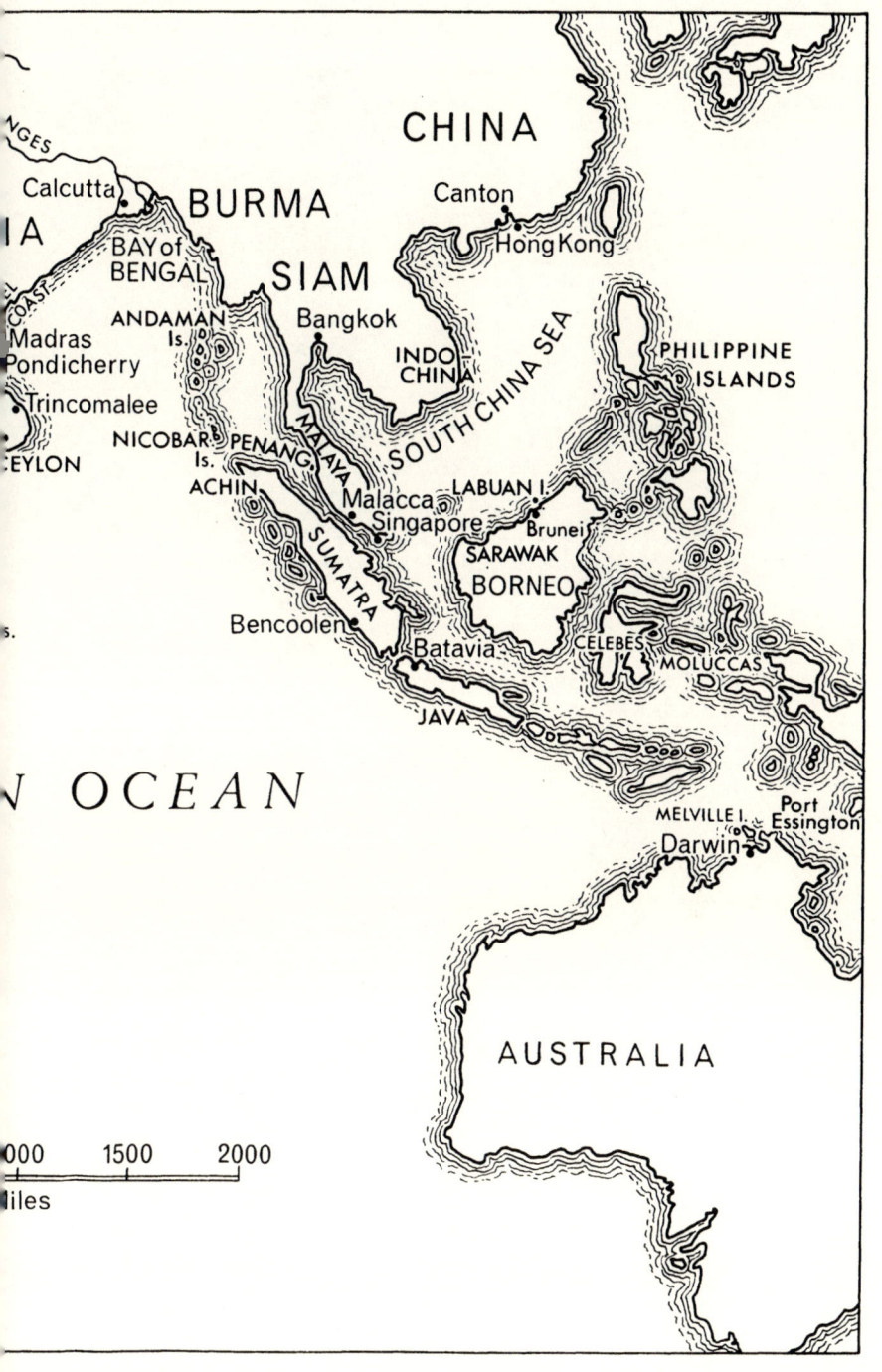

Cape to Canton

CHAPTER II

THE INDIAN OCEAN: FROM THE
CAPE TO CANTON

Unlike the Atlantic or the Pacific Oceans, the Indian Ocean is a land-locked sea—a gigantic bay of some 27 million square miles surrounded on three sides by land. On its northern Asiatic boundary lie two great bights—the Arabian Sea and the Bay of Bengal—both great highways of commerce for some three thousand years, and both governed in their sailing trades by the phenomenon of the monsoon. Further westward lie two arms of the Arabian Sea—the Persian Gulf leading to the Tigris–Euphrates valley and Mesopotamia, and the Red Sea accessible from the Gulf of Aden, through the narrow Straits of Bab-el-Mandeb. Eastward from the Bay of Bengal a second arm of the Indian Ocean extends southeastward between the west coast of the Malayan Peninsula and Sumatra. Protected at the western entrance by the Nicobar Islands and Penang, the strategically vital Straits of Malacca lead to the China Sea, and the gorgeous mosaic of the Indonesian Archipelago.

Alan Villiers once remarked that of the three great oceans, the Indian, on the whole, was 'always the most kindly to sailing ships'.[1] Certainly, for more than a thousand years before the intrusion of the Portuguese, trading fleets were putting out from Africa and south Arabian ports between April and September, when the monsoon wind blew from

[1] *The Indian Ocean* (London, 1952), p. 13.

31

the south-west;[1] thence a course of fifteen days or more brought them to the coast of India. In the days when seamanship had not progressed beyond the art of sailing with a fair wind, the advantages of crossing the Indian Ocean with the support of the prevailing monsoon are obvious; even out of sight of land, there was reasonable surety of reaching a fixed destination.

By the beginning of the Christian era seafaring communities, using outrigger vessels, had established trading routes that extended from the Eastern Archipelago to India, the shores of Arabia, the Red Sea and the African coast as far south as Madagascar.[2] With the end of the Roman era the Arab traders, who had been moving freely around the northern semi-circle of the Indian Ocean, found their way from the Red Sea to the Mediterranean, and thence, westward to the Pillars of Hercules. By about 1250 it is conceivable (although hardly likely) that they had rounded the Atlantic shoulder of North Africa, reaching as far southward as the Senegal river.[3]

To the eastward, after centuries of coasting around the Arabian Sea and the Bay of Bengal, they were cutting direct courses from Africa and India far beyond the boundaries of familiar waters. Steering by sun or the stars—for the eastern seafarer had a chart of the heavens long before the discovery of the magnetic compass—the Arab had become a confident

[1] The Arabs called these winds Mausim, meaning 'set-time'—a word which eventually developed into the standard colloquialism—monsoon.

[2] William Kirk, 'The N.E. Monsoon and Some Aspects of African History', *Journal of African History*, III, ii (1962), 265–7. The part played by Indian society in this early period of exploration trade and colonization is described briefly by Kirk in 'Indian Ocean Community', *Scottish Geographical Magazine*, LXVII, nos. 3–4 (December 1951), 163–4; see also G. B. Sansom, *The Western World and Japan*, pp. 43–4, 70–1.

[3] Cf. J. H. Rose, *Man and the Sea* (Cambridge, 1955), p. 61. Professor Charles Verlinden sees little evidence to support this speculation.

deep-water navigator. He was making voyages to the Spice Islands, Burma, Malaya and China, long before the first Europeans had burst their Mediterranean bounds and were pushing out into the central Atlantic, or down the west coast of Africa towards the Cape of Good Hope.

The great event of the fifteenth century, at least in the opinion of contemporaries, was not Columbus's discovery of America but Vasco da Gama's arrival at Calicut in India. Although the route was almost 4000 miles longer than that by way of the Mediterranean, his journey was made without the interruption of an isthmus or the danger of blockade by the capricious Ottoman Turks who had captured Constantinople in 1453. It should be remembered, however, that the opening of an all-sea route to India had been in preparation possibly for decades before da Gama set sail from Lisbon in 1497. In particular, recent research has revealed the manner in which Bartholomew Diaz blazed the trail to the Cape and opened the door to the East in 1487. In the words of a sixteenth century annalist: 'He saw the land of India but, like Moses and the Promised Land, was not allowed to enter therein.'[1]

Diaz and his fellow caravel captains not only made rough charts of the west coast of Africa, but more important, they were pioneers in the study of wind systems. They discovered that the central Atlantic favoured west-bound voyages; their observations made possible da Gama's run from the Cape Verde Islands to the edge of the South American continent, and thence, by means of the south-east trades and variables of the south Atlantic to the Cape. They laid down the 'rule of the road' in terms of Atlantic navigation, namely, to gain

[1] Quoted, Eric Axelson, *South-East Africa, 1488–1830* (London, 1940), p. 22.

favouring winds on the homeward as well as the outward journey, navigators must 'keep to the right'.[1]

Although Diaz pointed the way to India by sea, his tracings went little beyond Algoa Bay. What unknown barriers lay beyond, or to put it another way, how much did the Portuguese know about the south-east coast of Africa and the western Indian Ocean at the time when Vasco da Gama set out on his momentous voyage in the mid-summer of 1497? According to the experts, there is still room for conjecture; on the other hand, there is no argument about Portuguese intentions. In the same year that Diaz set out for the Cape, another small expedition had been despatched by way of the Mediterranean-Red Sea route to seek information about trade and coastal geography in eastern waters. The leader, Pedro da Covilhã, visited Calicut by way of the Persian Gulf, and then, in compliance with directions from the Portuguese monarch, he apparently followed the east African coast southward as far as Sofala. It is reasonable to believe, in the opinion of Professor Axelson, that the intelligence collected by Covilhã reached Portugal, and that it arrived some three years after Diaz had returned from the south Atlantic.[2] Covilhã had reported on the value of Calicut as a strategic trading port, and it is not, therefore, without significance that da Gama's instructions named Calicut as the destination —not just India.

[1] See Costa Brochado's highly coloured but useful survey of early Portuguese enterprise, *The Discovery of the Atlantic* (Lisbon, 1960), pp. 43, 78; see also, S. E. Morison, *Portuguese Voyages to America before 1500* (Cambridge, Mass., 1940). A summary of these early voyages is contained in Jean Poujade, *La Route des Indes et ses Navires* (Paris, 1946), ch. IV, 'Recherche et organisation de la Route du Cap pour Echapper au Controle de la Porte', but the best part of the book describes, with illustrations, the types of ships that were in use before the sixteenth century. [2] *Op. cit.* pp. 25–9.

Consequently, when da Gama doubled the Cape in November 1497 he was hardly entering unknown seas. On the other hand, he was the first seaman in history to complete, after infinite hardship, a voyage to India of some 9000 miles and to establish an efficient sailing track from Europe around the Cape of Good Hope, based on the movement of the trade winds and variables of the south Atlantic and the monsoons of the Indian Ocean north of the equator.[1] Nearly four centuries of sail were to confirm the rationality of his sailing directions and the quality of his seamanship.

After reaching Mozambique in March 1498 he pursued a cautious course northward to Kilwa and finally to Malindi 66 miles north of Mombasa; there on the advice of his Arab pilot, Ahmad Ibn-Madjid, probably the most learned navigator of the Indian Ocean,[2] he waited until the south-west monsoon was well advanced before starting the journey to Calicut. The lesson of this deliberate halt further contributed

[1] This track is approximately the same as that favoured today by the sailing directions of the British Admiralty and the United States' Hydrographic Office. See S. E. Morison, 'Sailing Directions of Vasco da Gama to Pedro Alvarez Cabral, 1500', *Mariner's Mirror*, XXIV, no. 4 (October 1938), 402.

[2] When Ibn-Madjid came on board, and was shown the astronomical instruments, including some wood and metal astrolabes, da Gama relates that 'the Moor did not manifest any astonishment as seeing such instruments...,' (J. C. Van Leur, *Indonesian Trade and Society: Essays in Asian Social and Economic History* (The Hague, 1955), p. 117). This is perhaps understandable when one realizes that this Moslem from Gujerat was responsible for thirty-five treatises on navigation. The most recently discovered of his *roteiros* or sailing directions have been published by the Russian, T. A. Chumovsky (ed.), *Três roteiros desconhecidos de Ahmad Ibn-Mādjid* (Lisbon, 1960); read before the Russian Academy of Sciences, 1957.

The Arabs produced many good pilot-guides, but the first reasonably accurate chart of the Indian Ocean does not apparently go back further than 1509. To the Portuguese, then, must go the credit for the first systematic effort at cartography; their *roteiros* 'laid the foundations of scientific navigation in the Indian Ocean'. See Toussaint, 'Archives of the Indian Ocean', *The Indian Ocean*, X (1956), p. 60.

to the European advance eastwards.[1] Had da Gama left the coast before the end of March, he would have found the north-east monsoon against him, and his only hope of reaching India (as his successors discovered) would have been to stand well over to the east before making his northing on or about the longitude of Ceylon.

Da Gama's epic voyage was the means of tying Europe directly by sea to the thoroughfares of the north Indian Ocean, and the consequences far exceeded those produced by all the overland expeditions to the East in previous centuries. Occurring almost simultaneously with the discovery of America, the opening of a Cape route was responsible for a revolutionary shift of power, wealth and possessions. Da Gama's achievement transferred to Lisbon, London and Amsterdam the strategic positions once occupied by the ancient cities of the Levant and Egypt; and, since she was first in the field, Portugal was able to stake out a virtual monopoly which she held for almost a hundred years.

From bases at Aden, Ormuz, Goa, Malacca and Mozambique the Portuguese soon obtained undisputed supremacy at sea, thus establishing a western hegemony in eastern waters. By the end of the nineteenth century the Indian Ocean had become the most Europeanized of all the world's seas, not excluding the Mediterranean. With the exception of Arabia, Persia and a relatively small section of north-east Africa, the encircling shores from the Cape of Good Hope half-way round the compass to Australia, as well as the islands between,

---

[1] A Greek by the name of Hippalus is assumed to have been the first European to record, in A.D. 45, that the winds in the general area of the Arabian Sea blew steadily in the same direction for almost the same number of months every year. Putting out to sea from Cape Fartak, he made a direct passage to the pepper-coast of Malabar.

were in the hands of Britons, French, Portuguese, Italians and Germans.[1]

In variety of routes and range of commerce, the Indian Ocean offered a striking contrast to that of the cloistered Mediterranean. The first European visitors who sailed round the Cape were surprised by what J. C. Van Leur has called 'the complete internationality of trade'.[2] 'After journeying through the inhospitable seas of southern Africa the Portuguese ships had come into regions where there was a complex of shipping, trade and authority as highly developed as the European: forms of political capitalism at least as large in dimensions as those of southern Europe, and probably larger; shipping in bottoms many of them carrying more than those used in European merchant shipping; a trade in every conceivable valuable high quality product carried on by a great multitude of traders; merchant gentlemen and harbour princes wielding as great financial power as did the merchants and princes of Europe....'[3] Like Alexandria, Constantinople, Venice and Genoa, great Indian ports such as Calicut and Cochin had risen to prosperity on the maritime enterprise of Arab traders, whose seamanship, navigation techniques and trading enterprise had long surpassed those of European peoples.[4]

[1] See Admiral G. A. Ballard, *Rulers of the Indian Ocean* (London, 1927), pp. 298–9.   [2] *Indonesian Trade and Society*, p. 111.

[3] *Ibid.* p. 117; quoted A. Toussaint, 'Archives of the Indian Ocean', p. 58.

[4] According to one contemporary estimate, there were some 15,000 foreign-trading Moslems in Calicut at the beginning of the fifteenth century. See O. K. Nambiar, *The Kunjalis, Admirals of Calicut* (London, 1963), pp. 15, 16, 29. See also G. B. Sansom, *The Western World and Japan*, pp. 55–7, 59–61.

Even after da Gama's successors brought more merchants, larger ships and bigger guns, the intricate pattern of trade in the Indian Ocean remained curiously unaltered. Despite rigorous Portuguese controls the traditional commercial framework existed essentially unchanged for another hundred years.

The Cape of Good Hope was the gateway to this fabulous empire; yet the Portuguese established no permanent settlement during their century-long ascendancy. Not until the Dutch began to spread their sails in the Indian Ocean did the Cape become a water and provisioning station, and not until the middle of the seventeenth century did Van Riebeeck begin to colonize it. The Dutch needed such a refreshment base because their main objective was usually the Spice Islands, and from the Cape to the Straits of Sunda, which separate Sumatra and Java, lies an immense expanse of water. The ill-conditioned fever-ridden vessels of the time[1]—uncoppered, poorly equipped, and often, after a month or so, short of provisions or water—could rarely withstand an uninterrupted voyage of five or six months.

By the end of the eighteenth century, however, improvements in shipbuilding and sailing techniques had greatly diminished the Cape's importance as a half-way house. It was safer and usually more economical to send the larger ships south-west in the direction of Rio de Janeiro rather than southward along the coast of Africa. From the great 'clearing house' of European shipping at the entrance to the Atlantic between Ushant and the south of Ireland, they could follow da Gama's wide triangular course from Madeira or the Canaries, past the Cape Verde Islands to within a hundred miles or more of the Brazilian coast. Thence, if there was no need of repairs or shortage of provisions, they could catch the south-east trades which gradually bore them into the region of the dependable westerlies—the 'Roaring Forties' in the lati-

---

[1] Throughout the eighteenth century, scurvy and fever remained the curse of the seas. As in da Gama's time, ships staggered into the Cape or St Helena not just decimated, but almost totally incapacitated by disease.

tude of 45 degrees. Finally, after passing the Cape, they might sail north by north-east through the Mozambique Channel to Ceylon or Bombay with the help of the south-west monsoon, or well to the eastwards of Madagascar where favouring winds allowed passage due north to Madras and Calcutta.[1]

Although the Cape remained a military rendezvous because of its proximity to converging Indian communication routes, once British forces had captured the port, as they did in 1795,[2] the strategic argument quickly evaporated, and at the barter which preceded the Peace of Amiens the British government preferred to surrender it and keep Ceylon. Napoleon's ill-fated Egyptian campaign had drawn public attention to the eastern Mediterranean, and statesmen who had recently been extolling the strategic advantages of the Cape were now busily searching for a more attractive 'key to the Indies'. Lord Nelson confirmed the trend of disillusionment with the salty weight of his experience and almost unchallengeable authority. The Cape, he pointed out, was a useful intermediary base in the old days, but with the introduction of coppered bottoms, Indiamen, like men-of-war, had less need to refit on a voyage to India. It had become no more than a pleasant 'tavern on the passage' which often delayed an ordinarily quick through-passage. Moreover, when the Dutch held it, you could buy a cabbage there for twopence; now, under the British, it cost a shilling.[3]

The fact of an established command of the sea helped to influence the surrender. Such a monopoly could not guaran-

[1] For an examination of alternative routes, see C. N. Parkinson, *Trade in the Eastern Seas* (Cambridge, 1937), especially chap. IV, 'The Eastern Seas'.

[2] In 1781 a British expedition would have occupied the base had it not been forestalled by the agile Suffren.

[3] Debate in the Lords on the Preliminaries of Peace, 3 November 1801 (*Parliamentary History of England*, XXXVI, 185).

tee the neutralization of the Cape, but it certainly minimized
the advantages of French possession. The Cape, like Mauritius, might still be of immense nuisance value to the French,
but it could not decide the fate of India. On the whole,
however, the strategic argument counted for little as compared with the economic; the decisive objection to retention
was the cost. The Cape of Good Hope was not regarded as a
commercial asset, and as a military base it might become an
increasingly heavy financial burden. In a country facing an
appalling burden of debt, peripheral defence issues disap-
peared in the gloom of Treasury accounting. The debates
in the Lords and the Commons were the first intimation of
the new climate of opinion that was to affect fundamentally
nineteenth-century imperial thinking. If the Dutch colony
were to be taken as a permanent possession, it must demonstrate that it could pay its way.

As it happened, with the resumption of war in September
1803, the shadow of Napoleon ceased to darken English
ledgers. Once again the 'expensive and unnecessary colony'
became the politician's 'key to India'. In a letter to the
Governor-General of India, Lord Castlereagh deftly glossed
the strategical *volte-face* that occurred between 1803 and the
second conquest of 1805: '...the true value of the Cape to
Great Britain is its being considered and treated at all times as
an outpost subservient to the protection and security of our
Indian possessions...its occupation is perhaps even more
material as depriving the enemy of the best intermediary
position between Europe and India, for assembling a large
European armament for service in the East Indies....'[1]

[1] Castlereagh to Cornwallis, 10 September 1805 (enclosed in Castlereagh to
the Lord Commissioners of the Admiralty, 10 September 1805; Ad. 1/4200).

On such negative grounds the statesmen of 1814 made their choice. They wanted to prevent the French from making use of a strategic base in time of war. Like Canada in 1763, the Cape appeared to be an unprofitable acquisition; Voltaire had voiced the opinion of the average Englishman as well as Frenchman when he wrote of the sterile frozen lands of cannibal savages, which had cost his country more money than all Canada was worth. In much the same language, an astute Dutch observer, Baron Van Pallandt, had condemned the Cape at the time of its return to Holland during the peace of Amiens as unworthy of the heavy sacrifices 'that continue to be made daily by the Republic'.[1] The 'best intermediary position between Europe and India' was a colonial luxury, but its occupation was now regarded as an unfortunate necessity. Thenceforward it was to be called by both armchair and professional strategists the 'key to the Indies', 'fortress of India', 'Master of Asia', the 'Gibraltar of India', among other clichés of history that were applied with equal abandon to St Helena, Mauritius, Madagascar, Ceylon, Penang, Aden and Singapore.

From 'the end of the world'—as some captains called the South African peninsula—the old Cape route crossed the Tropic of Capricorn to enter a primitive thinly populated and colonizable area, not important as a source of raw materials, but one which provided protective bases to overlook and secure the route. In the Indian Ocean proper, there is no wide-flung kaleidoscopic distribution of islands as in

[1] *General Remarks on the Cape of Good Hope* (1803); published in Cape Town, 1917, p. 9. The original French version is in Utrecht University Library. Van Pallandt called himself private secretary to the Governor and Commander-in-Chief, but his claim is not substantiated. See J. P. van der Merwe, *Die Kaap Onder die Bataafse Republick* (Amsterdam, 1926), p. 236 n. 1.

the Indonesian Archipelago; yet nature has spaced the stepping stones to India with a nice sense of utility, and the Napoleonic Wars had provided opportunities for the capture or cession of some of the more useful. Between the Cape and Bombay—a distance of some 4600 miles—lie Madagascar, Mauritius, the Comoro and Amirante Islands, and the Chagos, Seychelles and Maldive archipelagos. They represented a strategic chain of posts, whereby, as the *Quarterly Review* put it in 1830, 'our power in the eastern seas is to be maintained; and we cannot conceive that any more fatal blow could be levelled against our commercial greatness than would be effected by the relinquishment of these valuable dependencies'.[1]

North of the equator the route followed ancient thoroughfares to the riches of old and highly populated civilizations—Hindu, Buddhist and Moslem—to countries that offered the markets and the products which Europe had sought since the days of Vasco da Gama.[2] Eastward from Ceylon across the Bay of Bengal, a track of some 1300 miles from Colombo to Penang crossed an area equal to half Europe, with no convenient rendezvous west of the Andamans. Thence to Canton through the funnel of the Malacca Straits and into the China Sea lay a hazardous journey of nearly fifteen hundred miles, without a single harbour of refuge or a base from which the navy could operate against European rivals or Chinese and Malay pirates. Not until the occupation of the island of Labuan on the north-west coast of Borneo in 1846 was this gap partially filled.[3]

[1] XLII, 522–3.
[2] Jacques Auber, *Histoire de l'Ocean Indien* (Tananarive, Madagascar, 1955), pp. vii and 305.
[3] Graham Irwin, *Nineteenth Century Borneo: A Study in Diplomatic Rivalry* (The Hague, 1955), pp. 115–22.

In this fabled other-world of spikenard and cloves, pearls and pagodas, unicorns and elephants, flowering silks and shimmering odalisques, India was never a mere outpost. It was The Citadel—the principal headquarters of British dominion in the eastern seas. Projecting a thousand miles into the Indian Ocean, with Ceylon as its spearhead, this giant peninsula was becoming the strategic centre of a vast commercial network that included the Straits Settlements, the Indonesian Archipelago, China and Australia on the one hand, and on the other, Persia, Arabia, Egypt and East Africa. A British project of empire that had been initiated at the beginning of the seventeenth century, with a few coastal trading posts, had, by the beginning of the nineteenth century, developed into an elaborate organization of government, finance and communications based on London.

Trade in spices enforced by naval supremacy had been the simple policy of the Portuguese. Under their British successors this elementary traffic expanded to include luxury goods, indigo, jute, raw cotton, hemp and wheat in return for steadily increasing shipments of cotton textiles, and eventually, in the nineteenth century, the manufactured materials for railways, bridges and harbour installations. Through all the changes, from the first monopoly of the spice trade to the large-scale exports of capital and heavy equipment, the Indian economy became increasingly dependent on Europe, and Indian commerce almost completely dependent on maritime carriage. Indeed, a fundamental consideration in the history of India is the fact that from the sixteenth century onwards her future was determined at sea.[1] It was easy access by sea that had invited European conquest.

[1] K. M. Panikkar, *India and the Indian Ocean* (London, 1945; 2nd ed. 1951), pp. 83–4.

43

Physical facts prescribed that India should become an insular rather than a continental state. The very nature of India's frontiers made communication by land tedious and difficult. There can be no denying the strategic and commercial importance of the historic passes; the tribal invader had found convenient loopholes in the north-west and north-east; the mountains of Afghanistan and the Himalayas were penetrable to the enterprising merchant; but once the shattered empire of the Moguls succumbed to the European conqueror the sailing ship became the chief medium of European influence throughout the Indian Ocean and beyond. And because Indian economic life and commerce were tied to Europe by the sea, the Indian Ocean had become by the end of the Seven Years War essentially a British lake.

Until 1744 Britain had no squadron in East Indian waters; the French were first in the field; hence, La Bourdonnais's success off the Coromandel coast during the War of the Austrian Succession.[1] The first general action between the squadrons of Pocock and D'Ashé took place near Pondicherry in April 1758 when the Royal Navy gained command of the Bay of Bengal. During the War of American Independence the great Suffren fought Sir Edward Hughes to a draw in five fiercely contested battles, also off the Coromandel coast. The creditable French performance had little effect, however, on the outcome of the war in India. Of far greater significance for the future was the fact that successive engagements had been fought within an area extending some three hundred miles between the latitudes of Madras and the southern end of Ceylon. In other words, the west coast of India which

[1] See H. W. Richmond, *The Navy in the War of 1739-48* (3 vols., Cambridge, 1920), III, 179-83.

contained the principal harbour and dockyard of Bombay was no longer, as in the seventeenth century, adjacent to the main theatre of conflict. The strategic centre of gravity had shifted to the east coast, where not one harbour existed south of the unpopular Calcutta base up the Hooghli river.

The explanation lay in geography—the geography of the winds. Although favoured commercially by the alternating monsoons, India was strategically vulnerable during the north-east monsoon. Unpredictable hurricanes which had swept many British warships to disaster showed the terrible risks of wintering off Madras Roads. Consequently, between November and February, the Coromandel coast lay exposed to any enemy approaching from Malayan waters. Retreat to the west coast before the monsoon reached its height left the Bay of Bengal undefended against a hostile force launched from Achin or other ports to the eastward. A raiding squadron could reach its goal long before Bombay-based ships could reach the scene of trouble. Indeed, times of passage against an unfavourable monsoon might be multiplied six to eight times normal as a consequence of the awkward circuitous route, west and south of Ceylon, that had to be followed before a course could be laid to the east coast.

The Directors of the East India Company had long been convinced that Britain needed a base to the eastward which would make it possible to circumvent the deadly handicap of seasonal winds, as well as add to the security of the China trade. Shortly after the conclusion of the Seven Years War they began their search, investigating and appraising the old French Sumatran port of Achin, the Andamans, the Nicobars and Trincomalee in Ceylon. Not until 1786 did Captain

Francis Light, who was well acquainted with the Malayan coast of Kedah, and who was on friendly terms with its sultan, arrange on behalf of the company for the cession of an off-shore island about two-thirds the size of the Isle of Wight. Some fifteen miles long by nine broad, Prince of Wales Island, or Penang (as it was usually called) contained a spacious harbour formed by the strait (nearly two and a half miles wide) that separated its north-east extremity from the mainland of Kedah. In terms of India's defence, it was perfectly situated to command the Bay of Bengal and the Coromandel coast during the winter months when the warships of Bombay were held in durance by the north-east monsoon.

As it happened, however, neither as a naval establishment nor as a commercial entrepôt were the company's expectations realized. After Trafalgar, and particularly after the capture of Mauritius in 1810, the chief danger to Britain's eastern commerce was over; the heavy expenses of upkeep were no longer the inevitable price that had to be paid for the security of India's east coast. Moreover, Penang was too remote to tempt the bulk of the Indonesian Archipelago trade through the Dutch-controlled Straits. Faced with a deficit in their Indian budget, and under pressure of East India shipping interests at home, the Company refused to maintain the port as a naval base without Admiralty support.[1] This support was not forthcoming, and as a result the East Indies squadron was shortly reunited under one command based on Bombay. By 1830 Penang had become little more

---

[1] C. D. Cowan, 'Early Penang and the Rise of Singapore, 1805–1832', *Journal of the Malayan Branch of the Royal Asiatic Society*, XXIII, part 2, March 1950 (Singapore, 1950), p. 8.

than a watch-tower over the adjoining Malayan Peninsula, and a rendezvous for punitive expeditions against local pirates or the aggressive legions of imperial Siam.

Actually the abandonment of Penang as a naval base had been justified as early as 1796 by the acquisition of a more satisfactory all-year port equally capable of circumventing the handicap of the north-east monsoon. Lying to the southward of British settlements on the Coromandel coast, Trincomalee was neatly placed for rescue operations during either seasonal swing of the monsoon pendulum, and it offered, besides, the best land-locked harbour in the eastern seas. Although a Dutch possession for the great part of the eighteenth century, Trincomalee had played an important part in the defence of India. Both Boscawen and Hughes had used it not only for refitting and refreshment, but as a pivot of local naval strategy.[1] Trincomalee commanded both the Malabar and Coromandel coasts, and was in a better position to control the Bay of Bengal than Penang. Unlike the Cape, Ceylon provided an immediate safeguard against any enemy intrusion on the sub-continent. It was a real, not a fanciful key. '...in the hands of a powerful enemy', wrote Earl Macartney, the governor of the Cape, 'it might enable him to shake to the foundation, perhaps overturn and destroy the whole fabrick of our oriental opulence and dominion'.[2]

For the sake of India, therefore, Britain kept Ceylon at the peace. But farther to the east the policy of trade security seemed to be reversed. In 1794, when the French set up the Batavian Republic, Britain had responded quickly and

[1] See H. A. Colgate, *Trincomalee and the East Indies Squadron 1746–1844* (M.A. thesis, University of London, 1959), p. 479.

[2] To Henry Dundas, 10 July 1797 (G. M. Theal, *Records of the Cape Colony,* vol. II, December 1796 to December 1799 (Cape Town, 1898), p. 114).

characteristically by taking Malacca and the Dutch posts on the west coast of Sumatra. A year or so later, the Moluccas followed. With the renewal of war following the short-lived peace of Amiens, the surviving or restored remnants of the Franco-Dutch empire were picked up, not without considerable expense and trouble, one by one. At the end of 1810, the loss of the principal French base in the Indian Ocean —Ile de France (subsequently renamed Mauritius)—paved the way for the conquest of Java. By 1812 the Dutch empire was no more; Great Britain controlled the fate of every European settlement, base or coral islet in the eastern seas. She returned most of them to Holland.

In view of Britain's superiority at sea, there was, admittedly, no military advantage in territorial occupation, and very probably heavy financial loss to be expected in pacifying and administering proud and combative peoples, of whose varying cultures and histories most British ministers and officials were completely ignorant. None the less, while it may have been expedient to surrender territory, the treaty made no provision for the retention of a single British post on the most coveted trade channel in the eastern seas—the Straits of Malacca. The British flag still flew at Penang, and at Bencoolen on the western flank of Sumatra, but both were too remote to command the native trade of the Archipelago, or even to secure the Straits against pirates. Moreover, the restitution of Java in 1816 and Malacca two years later meant that the Dutch were in a tactical position to control two vital approaches to the Archipelago and the China Sea—the Straits of Sunda as well as of Malacca. A reinvigorated or a French-dominated Holland might, in time of war, temporarily cut the main trade route between India and China.

'Through mistaken generosity', declared the *Quarterly Review*, Britain had 'lavished everything upon this ungrateful people....'[1]

For good reasons of expediency, however, British statesmen were concerned about cultivating the friendship of a rival who happened also to be France's continental neighbour. Indeed, British policy towards the Netherlands empire was almost entirely a consequence of European geography—or to put it another way, of British policy towards France in Europe. Lord Castlereagh, the Foreign Secretary, preferred to maintain Britain's traditional course—the support of the Dutch as a barrier against the power of France in Europe as well as overseas. In the interests of British naval supremacy and trade security he was willing to keep certain vital bases— Malta, the Cape, Mauritius and Ceylon and to limit the French to a purely commercial occupation of their few East Indies factories; but he was insistent on recovering Dutch goodwill by a peace of reconciliation and restoration. In following this course, he was indirectly responsible for a territorial settlement that was both a rebuff and a challenge to the British merchant and industrialist.

It is customary to applaud Castlereagh's shrewd and generous policy of restraint. Yet even Sir Charles Webster would confess that he lacked both the capacity and the will to seek public support for his policies. Castlereagh seems to have assumed that a resolute direction of foreign policy would in the long run evoke popular acquiescence; in other words, that public opinion (which he did not disregard) could be pressed into reluctant acquiescence even against the pressures of new vested interests. While admitting the wisdom of

[1] XLII (1830), 438.

restraint in the face of huge territorial temptations, it is none the less clear that he underestimated the growing compulsions of the factory age, reflected in the growth of middle class political liberalism, which he both feared and distrusted.

The presence of a new force in English life was already disturbing traditional calculations based on personal connections between European rulers.[1] Naturally the diplomatic minuet of advances and strategic retreats, bluffs and double-bluffs continued; they were an essential part of the tactics of European national life. But policies made in Whitehall tended increasingly to be diverted, adjusted or even profoundly altered by the actions of trading and industrial classes who resented Castlereagh's apparent anti-liberalism in domestic matters. Indeed, the vested interest was rapidly becoming the national interest; the 'nation of shopkeepers' was becoming the industrial workshop of the world.

Pressures to increase British export trade were growing daily; and the new generation of 'go-getters' was concerned with gaining access to new sources of supply as well as new markets. In so far as their ambitions had imperial or territorial implications, these derived almost entirely from the fact that conquest or political domination meant security against the adverse trade competition of a rival. British merchants wanted to sell or buy in tropical areas on at least as good terms as any other European country. Hence, they were shocked to learn that the new peace treaty offered not guarantees of freedom, but barriers to expanding commerce. At the expense of the private trader—for the East India Company had lost its monopoly in 1813—the British government intended to encourage Holland to rebuild her Asian

[1] See *The Foreign Policy of Castlereagh 1815–1822* (London, 1925), pp. 496–7.

empire, regardless of the fact that the Dutch might oust British trade from Indonesian waters and possible beyond.

As it happened, Castlereagh's magnanimity did nothing to melt Dutch commercial hearts or diminish their imperial aspirations.[1] Supported by a mere handful of small warships, Holland was ready, within four years of the peace, to shut Indonesian ports to British shipping, and to renew treaties with independent local chiefs.[2] She was clearly aiming at preventing Britain from winning a foothold in any strategic area alongside or within the Archipelago that might interfere with her effort at commercial monopoly. And however earnest the British policy of cherishing the Low Countries for fear of France, the greatest industrial and naval power in the world was hardly likely to continue indefinitely to tolerate an obstinately exclusive colonial policy on the part of a minor state that she herself had helped to rehabilitate.

In August 1819 Lord Castlereagh informed the British ambassador at The Hague that the government would not 'acquiesce in a practical exclusion, or in a mere permissive toleration, of British commerce throughout the immense extent of the Eastern Archipelago; nor can they consent to expose the direct commerce of this country with China to all the disadvantages which would result, especially in time of war, from all the military and naval keys of the Straits of Malacca being exclusively in the hands of the Netherlands Government'.[3] In the circumstances, it is not surprising that

---

[1] Note in this connection the cryptic estimate of Professor P. J. Blok, 'England and Holland at the beginning of the Nineteenth Century', *English Historical Review*, XXIX (1914), 331.

[2] C. E. Wurtzburg, *Raffles of the Eastern Isles* (London, 1954), p. 434; C. D. Cowan, *Nineteenth Century Malaya* (London, 1961), p. 6.

[3] Quoted Irwin, *Nineteenth Century Borneo*, pp. 56–7.

the Governor-General of Bengal should have stressed the vital necessity in the face of a growing Dutch exclusion policy, of establishing 'a station beyond Malacca, such as may command the southern entrance to those Straits'.[1]

Early in December 1818, with the blessing of Lord Hastings, Stamford Raffles had set off from Calcutta for Penang, and a couple of weeks later, unbeknown to the administration, he embarked for the Karimun Islands at the southern end of the Straits of Malacca. On 29 January 1819 he hoisted the East India Company's flag on a small and unimportant possession of the Malay empire of Johore, called Singapúra.

Wedged within the Malacca bottleneck between Sumatra and the Malay peninsula, Singapore is a low almost flat pancake of an island, which was then covered, like the neighbouring jig-saw of islets, with thick jungle to the water's edge. It is separated from the extremity of the Peninsula by a narrow alley of water, now bridged by a causeway less than half a mile long. When Raffles first landed, there were probably fewer than 150 inhabitants—fishermen, pirates, possible traders and a few representatives of the sultan's local ruler, the Data' Temenggong. It must have taken imagination as well as considerable courage for even an impetuous and naturally insubordinate Company officer to commandeer so uninviting a 'key' to empire. The island was unkempt, and unhealthy, and the romantic discovery of fragments of some bygone citadel in no way relieved an atmosphere of dank desolation and decay. Yet Raffles had no doubts that he could restore ancient Singapore 'to her old magnificence'.[2] With this single station, he wrote a friend, 'I would under-

---

[1] Lady Raffles, *Memoir of the Life and Public Services of Sir T. S. Raffles* (London, 1830), p. 369.   [2] *Ibid.* p. 454.

take to counteract all the plans of Mijnheer; it breaks the spell, and they the Dutch are no longer the exclusive sovereigns of the Eastern Seas'.[1]

Raffles intended that Singapore should be the Malta of the East,[2] but a Malta which, in an era of expanding shipping and industry, would be the means of extending British influence and commerce eastward. Equidistant from the most important commercial cities in western and eastern Asia, Calcutta and Canton, it would be the military fulcrum of the British imperial position eastward of India. Secured against all European threats by the power of the navy, it could be the ultimate instrument for extending British trade and influence in distant waters. Eastward of the Cape there was not a single foreign port from which an enemy squadron could challenge Britain's command of the Indian Ocean.[3] As a potential naval base, Singapore commanded the entrance to the Straits as effectually as Gibraltar controlled the entrance to the Mediterranean; and it was in a position to exert a far greater influence on the trade and navigation of the China Sea and the eastern Indian Ocean than Malta ever exercised on the eastern Mediterranean.[4]

---

[1] *Ibid.* p. 377.   [2] *Ibid.* p. 380.

[3] The French island of Bourbon was not comparable in harbour facilities with the former base, Ile-de-France (Mauritius).

[4] In fact, Singapore remained a minor naval base until the outbreak of World War I, less well provided than Simonstown, not to speak of Halifax and Bermuda. A small 'Patent Slip and Dock at the New Harbour' was in operation by 1860, but not until August 1913 was the large 'King's Dock' (873 ft × 93 ft with a depth of 30 ft 9 in. over the sill) finally opened. See Walter Makepeace, 'The Port of Singapore' and Sir John Rumney, 'The Tanjong Pagar Dock Company' in W. Makepeace, G. E. Brooke and R. St J. Braddell (eds.), *One Hundred Years of Singapore* (2 vols., London, 1921), I, 578–92; II, 1–19. See also Dominions Royal Commission, *Memoranda and Tables as to the Chief Harbours of the British Empire and Certain Foreign Countries* (London, 1917), which compare the harbour facilities of Aden, Bombay, Calcutta, Colombo, Hong Kong and Singapore (pp. 79–90).

Albuquerque had recognized the strategic importance of a Straits base when he captured Malacca for the Portuguese in 1511, and Malacca became a principal emporium for the spice trade of the Archipelago. But this interest, although inherited, was not cherished by Britain. In the nineteenth century, the East India Company had lost its old enthusiasm for the Archipelago as a producer of staples, partly owing to their loss of monopoly privileges in 1813, but chiefly because the China tea trade had developed in staggering proportions compared with the traditional spice trade. Indeed, the renunciation of British interest in Indonesian waters was demonstrated not only by the surrender of Java in 1816, but—and far more conclusively—by the Anglo-Dutch treaty which Canning negotiated in 1824, wherein Britain, by a self-denying commitment, undertook to establish no settlements on any of the islands south of the Straits of Singapore.[1] In return, the Dutch abandoned all claims to Singapore, ceded Malacca, and agreed to abstain from interference in the Malayan Peninsula which was vaguely assumed to be under British protection. So long as the route to China was adequately safeguarded, Britain was willing to appease the Netherlands by renouncing any policy of territorial or trade expansion in Indonesian waters. The empire of the East Indies could stay with the Dutch as long as they left the route to China alone.

It is not my purpose to discuss either the phenomenal growth of Singapore as a trading entrepôt, or the prolonged

---

[1] Curiously enough, in his *Foreign Policy of Canning* (London, 1925), H. W. V. Temperley makes no mention of this treaty, or of preceding developments going back to 1817 when Canning was at the Board of Control. For a detailed discussion of these negotiations leading to 1824, see Nicholas Tarling, *Anglo-Dutch Rivalry in the Malay World, 1780-1824* (Cambridge, 1962), pp. 82, 113, 115-24 and chap. 5, 'The Treaty of 1824', pp. 133-73.

and bitter disputes which followed the introduction of Dutch punitive and prohibitive tariffs after 1824. Despite the safeguards written into the Treaty, the Dutch did their best during the next twenty-five years to damage the British-China trade.[1] There was chronic friction, but there was no shooting. The only serious incident that might have temporarily disrupted the eastern trade routes occurred in November 1830, when the Belgians declared for independence, and subsequently excluded the House of Orange from the throne. France was prepared to intervene, and offered the Duc de Nemours as candidate for the new monarchy. Fortunately, none of the major powers wanted war, and a Congress which sat in London finally settled that Belgium should become neutral and independent under Prince Leopold of Saxe-Coburg-Gotha. However, the Dutch refused to accept the judgment, and Leopold's untimely suggestion that Luxemburg be added to his kingdom provided an excuse for intervention. Early in August 1831 they invaded Belgium, and only the advance of the French army into Belgium saved Brussels.[2] The British fleet was ordered to the Scheldt, and with the assistance of French troops blockaded Antwerp fortress.

Once again as during the Napoleonic Wars the East India Company faced the prospect of organizing convoys in defence of the China trade. A general embargo was laid on all Netherlands shipping, and commanders of ships in every

[1] Tarling, *Anglo-Dutch Rivalry*, chap. v; L. A. Mills, *British Malaya, 1824–1867* (Singapore, 1925), pp. 71–5; Cowan, *Nineteenth Century Malaya*, pp. 22 ff.; J. S. Furnivall, *Netherlands India, A Study of Plural Economy* (Cambridge, 1944), pp. 129–30, 171.

[2] Temperley and Penson, *Foundations of British Foreign Policy, From Pitt (1792) to Salisbury (1902)* (Cambridge, 1938), p. 89.

station were ordered to waylay any merchant vessel bearing the Dutch flag. An embargo was not, of course, a declaration of war; it conferred no belligerent rights. On the other hand, Holland might have attempted reprisals short of war by sending out privateers or issuing *letters of marque*;[1] consequently, Vice-Admiral Gore, the commander-in-chief of the East Indies squadron, had to act quickly to warn and to protect trade moving towards the Straits of Malacca.[2]

As it happened, such precautions proved unnecessary. Even when the news of the commercial blockade and the bombardment of Antwerp reached Java in the spring of 1833, there was no disposition on the part of the Dutch authorities to molest British shipping in or near their Indonesian ports. Gore corresponded politely with the Dutch Governor-General; the amenities were maintained in word and deed, and even the pirates showed a sympathetic lack of aggressiveness during the crisis.[3] None the less, it was a great relief to both the British admiral and the Dutch governor, when the long-awaited mails arrived with news that Antwerp had finally surrendered to the allies, and had been handed over to Belgium in May 1833.

Thenceforward, until the end of the century, British routes to India and China were never even threatened by a major naval incursion. Other European nations might maintain fragments of empire—Portugal in Mozambique and on the coast of India, Holland in the Indonesian Archipelago, the

---

[1] J. Barrow, Secretary of the Admiralty, to the Secretary of the Board of Control (encl. in Grant to Sir James Graham, 7 November 1832), Admiralty, 5 November 1832 (Ad. 1/3919).

[2] See Gore to Elliot, 19 April 1833 (no. 30), enclosing Gore to Earl of Clare, Gov.-in-Council, Bombay, 9 April 1833 (Ad. 1/211).

[3] Gore to Elliot, Madras, 23 September 1833 (no. 100) (Ad. 1/212).

Arabs in Zanzibar and the French in Bourbon, Madagascar and ultimately Indo-China; but at no time did their existence affect British command of the Indian Ocean.

Moreover, it was Britain's happy lot to have no contiguous frontiers with other European powers in Asia; consequently the chances of sudden diplomatic incidents were rare. Only in the event of a great power approaching within threatening proximity of India was the Foreign Office likely to consider force as a remedy. And on only one occasion when French gunboats blockaded Bangkok in 1893 were fears aroused that the subjugation of Siam by France might bring Indo-China into undesired neighbourhood with Burma and India. 'In all this matter we have only one prime interest', wrote Lord Rosebery to Queen Victoria at the height of the Siamese crisis. 'It is to keep a buffer between the French frontier and that of India, in order that a vast expenditure and danger may not be incurred by the immediate proximity of a great military power on our South-Eastern flank.'[1] For a moment in 1893 the situation was critical, and a collision seemed inevitable. Fortunately, the officer commanding the British flotilla discovered in time that he had misunderstood the orders of the French admiral, and the incident was closed.[2] Although this was the year of the Naval Scare, the Admiralty were unperturbed; in the event of war, the Foreign Office counted on the support of both Italy and Germany.

Because Britain remained generally confident of her naval superiority *vis-à-vis* France and Russia, the influence of a parsimonious Exchequer on broad naval strategy tended to be considerable, if not paramount. Admiralty Lords during the

[1] The Marquess of Crewe, *Lord Rosebery* (2 vols., London, 1931), II, 424-6.
[2] *Ibid.* p. 425; also A. G. Gardiner, *The Life of Sir William Harcourt* (2 vols., London, 1923), II, 240-1.

latter half of the nineteenth century tended to accept the Foreign Office aphorism—let satisfied dogs sleep. Bases, like overseas squadrons, were therefore at the mercy of Treasury hatchetmen. While Singapore and Bombay could flourish as great commercial entrepôts on main lines of traffic, in an age of comparative peace strictly naval installations like Simonstown or Trincomalee had become expensive anomalies. Indeed, the popular absorption of Free Trade principles seemed to have had a soporific effect on military thinking. Englishmen, in the opinion of Admiral Owen, were becoming careless of strategic values.[1] Britain's supremacy at sea was indisputable; India was safe; Simonstown could be left to the care of the Colonial Office, and Trincomalee to the encroaching jungle.

The conditions imposed by British politics in the mid-Victorian age did not encourage either the upkeep of old, or the development of new British bases. In the judgment of many politicians—and not only Liberals like Gladstone—the introduction of order in primitive lands, however noble the intention and however worthy the consequences, eventually led to territorial additions which tended to expand in the interests of preserving order. *Laisser-faire* should favour a salutary negligence. Britain, it was urged, had more than enough on hand; the consolidation of present responsibilities was burden enough without the acquisition of new colonial territories, even for such respectable purposes as winning markets in areas that had once been the preserve of the Dutch and the Spanish.

On the other hand, it is not difficult to imagine the effects on East Indies commerce had there been no bases and no

[1] Owen to Elliot, 5 October 1831 (Ad. 1/205).

patrolling warships to check piracy. The presence of even two or three sloops cruising in the Malacca Straits or along the west coast of the Malayan Peninsula bolstered confidence among the trading community, European, Chinese and native, and certainly discouraged any major operations by pirates. In the later thirties, both the Foreign Office and the Admiralty had shown an increasing awareness of growing British responsibilities in the East, and the occupation of Hong Kong in 1841 had securely fixed a military terminus for the China route from Singapore. But throughout the long stretch of some 1500 miles there was no port of inter-mediate communication, no base from which the Royal Navy could operate against Chinese or Malay pirates, and no har-bour whence shipping could take shelter from the typhoons and hurricanes of the South China Sea.

The foundation of successive settlements in northern Australia—Melville Island, Raffles Bay and finally Port Essington in 1838—suggested the need not only for a com-manding military post, but 'a central point of commerce' to offset Dutch influence and authority in a lucrative trading area, still partly paralysed by the ravages of pirates. Neither the British government, nor the East India Company, had any intention of being hustled into new territorial adventures; on the other hand, there was an equal determination to prevent any other power—Spain, Holland, France or even the United States—from occupying positions which Britain herself had no wish to annex. In 1824 Britain had accepted the Dutch pretensions to hegemony within the Archipelago. There-after, however, the discontents of commercial interests, com-bined with growing apprehensions about Dutch ambitions, had produced an uneasy stalemate.

It is probably fair to say that the balance between acquiescence and intervention teetered uneasily until the first China War threw Hong Kong on the scales. Less than a year later, a minor province of the sultan of Brunei—Sarawak—was ceded to James Brooke 'with all its revenues and dependencies'. The advantages of a connecting link between Borneo and the China coast were obvious. A base on Borneo's north coast, wrote the commander-in-chief of the newly instituted China squadron, Rear-Admiral Sir Thomas Cochrane, could control 'the shortest and best road to the China market on the one hand and the East India on the other'.[1]

In the end, after much exploration and much debate, the island of Labuan which James Brooke had obtained from the sultan of Brunei in 1844 was the British government's choice. The discovery of coal in the vicinity reinforced the Admiralty's opinion that Labuan was the most suitable harbour for the suppression of piracy and the establishment of a permanent commercial ascendancy over the Dutch. In July 1846, despite the opposition of Gladstone and his friends who were deeply averse to 'the multiplication of colonies at the other end of the world', the Island was accepted as a Crown Colony and naval base to be administered by the Colonial Office. Hailed as a Singapore in miniature, Labuan as a commercial entrepôt failed utterly to achieve the hopes of its supporters. None the less, it served its purpose as a strategic sentry-box. The occupation of the hermaphrodite base 'something more than a station, and something less than a colony', completed the strategic chain of posts that ran from the Cape to the China coast.

---

[1] To Secretary of the Admiralty, 27 August 1845 (no. 146) (Ad. 1/5561).

The Indian Ocean: From the Cape to Canton

Since the days of Vasco da Gama the Indian Ocean had been the hunting ground of European nations. Over a span of four hundred years, command of European waters had meant paramountcy in the Indian Ocean. From the sixteenth century onwards, control of the main theatre in and about the English Channel had implied the containment of rival European powers. The defeat of Spain, then Holland and finally, after a century-long duel, France had meant consistent British command of Atlantic outlets to other seas; the control of the Atlantic was almost simultaneously applicable to the Indian Ocean. Such oceanic hegemony—if I may use a somewhat ponderous phrase—made it possible for Britain to bring her strength to bear on any point of the globe that touched salt water. The achievements of La Bourdonnais on the Coromandel Coast, or the brilliant strokes of Suffren, had been of little avail in the final result, so long as Anson and Hawke, Rodney or Nelson could win victories in the Atlantic, and thus permit the tide of British ascendancy to sweep around the Cape. In other words, India's military attachment to Great Britain was a direct consequence of British command of the English Channel.[1] A small emergency naval force, the East India squadron—usually less than a dozen sloops and frigates with occasionally a ship-of-the-line—was insufficient to quell the ubiquitous pirates and slavers, but as a symbol it was potent enough to keep the Indian Ocean a *mare clausum* to major hostile forces.

By the end of the nineteenth century, however, the unique predominance of the Mistress of the Atlantic was coming to

[1] See in this connection A. T. Mahan, *The Problem of Asia and its Effect upon International Policies* (Boston, 1900), p. 27; also Kirk, 'Indian Ocean Community', *Scottish Geographical Magazine*, LXVII (December 1951), 162.

an end. Britain's industrial lead was being overtaken by both Japan and the United States, and the rise of these two industrial nations made the Pacific Ocean automatically a nursery of sea power and a vital area of strategical movement. With the development of an American navy in the Pacific, and a powerful Japanese navy on the outskirts of the Indian Ocean, a long-established axiom was about to be extinguished.

Hitherto by commanding the seas bordering the Atlantic frontier of western Europe, Britain had been able to maintain not only her own security but that of her far-flung colonial possessions. By 1914 with greater naval forces than she had ever before possessed she was compelled to renounce or farm out her overseas commitments, in order to concentrate her strength in and about the North Sea. Atlantic supremacy was no longer identical with two-hemisphere supremacy. Early in 1942 when the Japanese captured Singapore, bombed Darwin and threatened the conquest of the intervening shores and islands, a British monopoly of the Indian Ocean had finally come to an end.

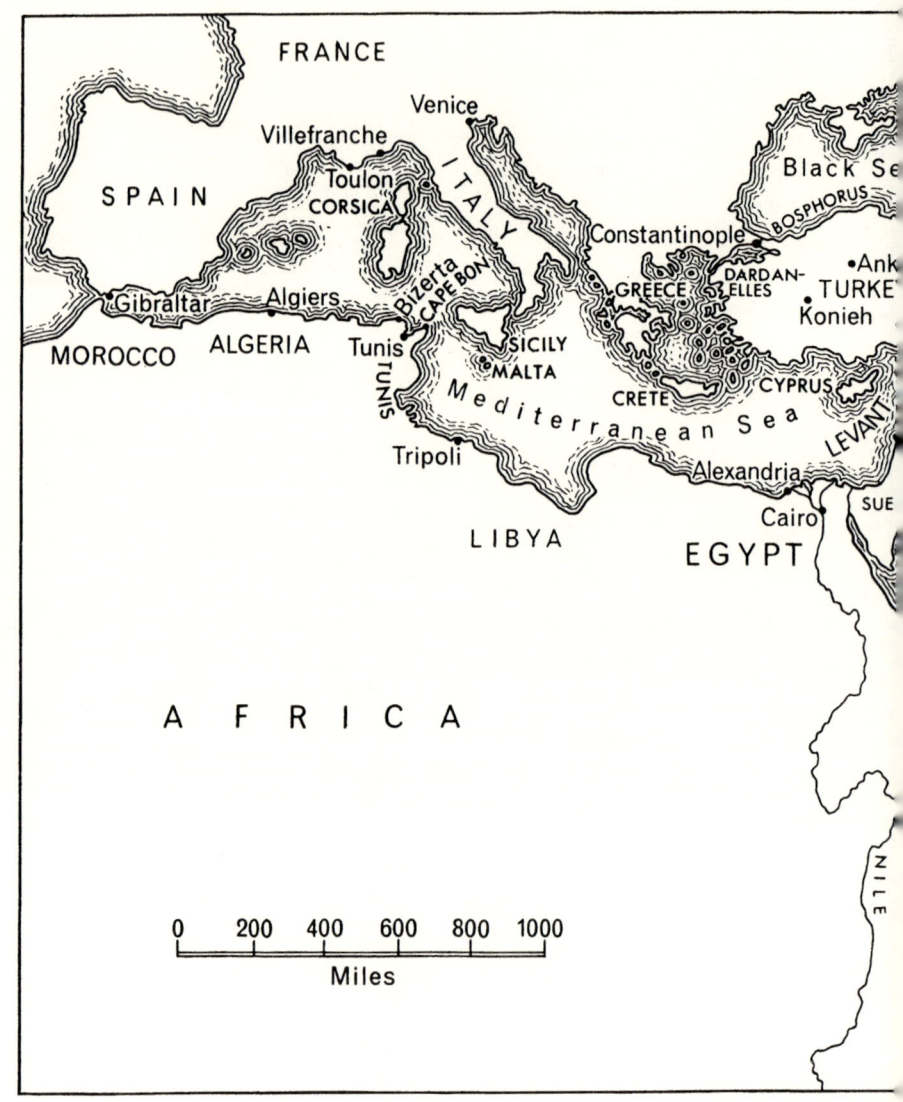

The Mediterranean (

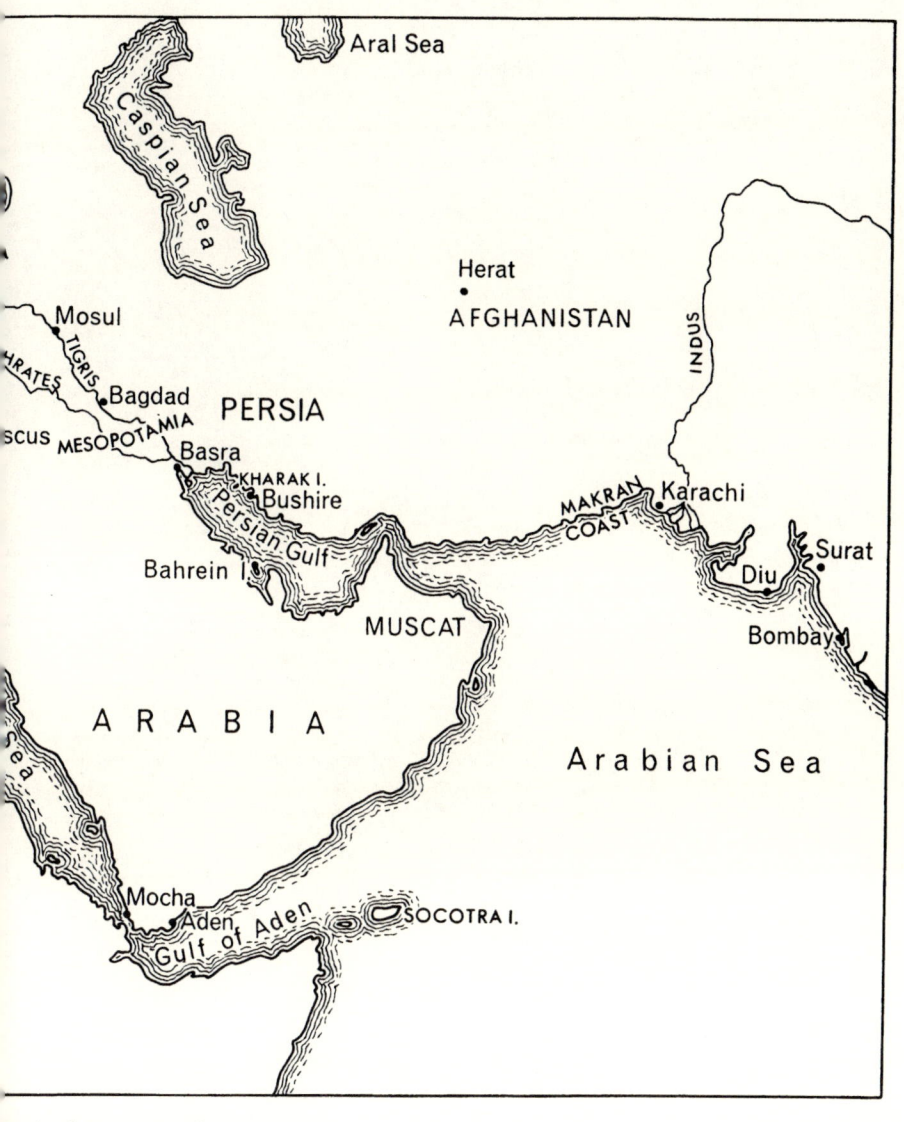

Gibraltar to Bombay

CHAPTER III

THE MEDITERRANEAN CORRIDOR: GIBRALTAR TO BOMBAY

Pondering the future of sea power in 1902, Admiral Mahan made bold to prophesy that the Mediterranean could be 'either the seat of one dominant control, reaching thence in all directions, owning a single mistress', or the scene of a continual competitive struggle.[1] 'The distant East,' he went on, 'in whatever spot there hostilities may rage, will represent, will be, the offensive sphere; but the determination of the result, in case of prolongation of war, will depend upon control of the Mediterranean.'

Mahan miscalculated the eastward shift of strategic power from European waters, but his first dictum was well founded. As the arena of competitive imperial struggles, going back beyond Rome and Carthage, the Mediterranean holds a unique place in history. From ancient times its commercial tributaries extended overland to the Euphrates and the Persian Gulf, as well as southward to the Red Sea across an insignificant tract of Egyptian sand that tied the vast Eurasian continent to the compact mass of Africa. Phoenicians and Assyrians, Greeks, Romans and Arabs had successfully exploited these highways to enlarge their wealth and buttress their power. To Alexander the Great, Ptolemy Philadelphus, Napoleon and Nelson, the Isthmus and Egypt represented the vital hinge between East and West.

After the conquest of Egypt in 332 B.C., Alexander built

[1] *Retrospect and Prospect* (London, 1902), p. 162.

the city of his name as principal entrepôt for the Red Sea traffic; and under the Ptolemies who succeeded him a few years later Alexandria became the most important commercial city in the world.[1] A canal seems to have been planned to run directly across the Isthmus from sea to sea to replace the circuitous and silted canal and river system of the Pharaohs; but the project was abandoned on the assumption that the higher level of the Red Sea would lead to destructive inundations on Mediterranean shores.[2] As late as the eighth century the ancient waterway was intermittently maintained; but not long after the Arab conquest of Egypt all routes to the East from the Mediterranean, whether by land or water, fell into decline until revived by the Venetians in the later middle ages. As it happened, however, the fall of Constantinople in 1453 created new obstacles until forty-five years later the Portuguese provided an escape from Turkish intransigence by establishing a new route around the Cape of Good Hope. The consequent shift of power and energy from the Mediterranean to the Atlantic presented western European powers with a virtual monopoly of the oriental trade. After some 2000 years the old 'overland' route that had helped to sustain the prosperity of successive empire and city states had ceased to flourish.

Not until the eighteenth century did Europe regain serious interest in the abandoned corridor. With the growth of Indian commerce and the accompanying Anglo-French rivalry, the short route to India was rediscovered. During

[1] See Jean Poujade, *La Route des Indes et ses Navires*, pp. 71–3. For a general outline of ancient routes see chap. II, 'Création, Ouverture, Développement et Fermeture de la Porte Sud de la Méditerranée sur l'Extrême Orient'.

[2] This belief persisted well into the nineteenth century. See Hugh J. Schonfield, *The Suez Canal in World Affairs* (London, 1952), pp. 3–4, 21.

the Seven Years War, political imperialism supported commercial ambition; the flag retraced old paths of trade, and the connection held until Napoleon's Egyptian adventure followed by unsettled political conditions in the early years of the nineteenth century made it hazardous and unprofitable.[1] Only after the rise of Mehemet Ali as virtual ruler of Egypt did both Alexandria, and the Red Sea route it served, return to active, though precarious life.

British interest in this ancient highway, which had been stimulated by Napoleon's adventures in Egypt, was quickened by the advent of steam in the late twenties, and consolidated in the thirties by fear of French and Russian political designs and military aggressions. Dominating all political discussions of Near East problems was the fear that Egypt and the Levant might fall into hostile hands and bar the land roads between London and Bombay. All the main foreign policy decisions that were made in respect of the Ottoman empire were influenced by, if not based on, the fact that these and adjoining provinces lay athwart the corridor that linked England with the East; and however meagre the total of serviceable men-of-war in an era of parsimony and peace, lines of communication to India conditioned the normal distribution of British naval forces outside home waters. Russian intervention in Turkey or in Persia, or a successful French intrigue in Egypt was sufficient to impel Britain to the verge of war, as demonstrated by the chain of successive crises symbolized by such names as Constantinople, Aden,

[1] News of the war with France in 1778, and again in 1793, reached Calcutta, by way of the Red Sea, a considerable time before the French in India were informed. Following the French occupation of Egypt between 1798 and 1801, a British mail service was resumed. See H. L. Hoskins, *British Routes to India* (London, 1928), pp. 21–5, 88–9.

Bagdad, Herat and Kharak. Indeed, Britain was prepared in a pinch to fight both France and Russia to keep her Mediterranean corridor intact.

'Of all our scattered possessions', wrote a typical political commentator of 1851, 'the mightiest in importance as well as extent is incontestably our Indian Empire.... And yet, but for one circumstance she [Britain] would have half the circuit of the globe to make, to communicate with it. That one circumstance is the Transit across Egypt.'[1] To put it more precisely, some ninety miles of sand blocked a water route that would otherwise have permitted continuous steam voyage from Portsmouth to Bombay in little more than six weeks.

But the isthmus was also a bridge that obviated—at least for mails, bullion and passengers—a journey of possibly four months. From Alexandria where early Victorian tourists wisely retreated before the scruffy mob of half-naked Arabs that awaited the arrival of the steam packet from Falmouth, the freight was conducted to the banks of the Mahmoudie Canal. Thence the journey was continued some forty miles by canal boat or barge to Atfeh on the Nile, and finally up the Nile some 120 miles to Cairo—a stage which usually took about sixteen hours. From there, unguarded except for Bedouin drivers and one or two guides, who acted as traffic rather than security officers, camel convoys pursued their nonchalant way to the Red Sea.[2] On one occasion at least it was estimated that 3000 camels were employed to carry the £400,000 cargo of a single steamer across the Isthmus.[3] To

[1] Anon. *The Present Crisis in Egypt* (London, 1851), p. 4.
[2] After 1840, springless carriages and vans began to replace the camels and the donkeys as passenger transport (Hoskins, *op. cit.* p. 237).
[3] J. Russell Smith, *Industrial and Commercial Geography*, new ed. (New York, 1925), p. 794.

the merchant of the city whose eyes were concentrated on the India post and the safety of hundreds of small boxes of dollars and sovereigns that crossed the desert with no other protection than camel drivers and British prestige, any step likely to disturb the tranquillity of Egypt might be disastrous. Is it seriously proposed, declared a member of the House of Lords with biting irony at the beginning of the Near East crisis of 1839, 'to make an independent monarchy of Egypt, and break up the Turkish Empire to facilitate our Indian mails?'[1]

Unfortunately, the Mediterranean corridor was highly vulnerable. Rival nations lay along or in proximity to its indented shores, and some of them possessed good harbours and strong bases. Local naval superiority on the part of one hostile state could break the line of communication. The physical peculiarities of the Mediterranean enhanced this danger. Three straits were of decisive importance—Gibraltar, at the Atlantic entrance, the bottleneck between Cape Bon in Africa and the toe of Sicily, and the Dardanelles which permitted Russian access from the Bosphorus and Black Sea. The effect of these narrow passages (particularly the Sicilian, as we know from World War II) was to favour the tactics and strategy of contiguous Mediterranean powers.[2] Consequently the security of the Mediterranean route demanded not only aggregate superiority over any potential European enemy, but also the possession of such convenient and capacious ports as would enable a British squadron to hold or neutralize an enemy concentration until reinforcements

---

[1] T. A. Curtis, *State of the Question of Steam Communication with India, via the Red Sea, etc.* (London, 1839), p. 31.

[2] On the geography of the coasts, as well as currents, tides, winds and weather, see Rear-Admiral W. H. Smyth, *The Mediterranean: A Memoir—Physical, Historical and Nautical* (London, 1854).

arrived from home waters. Ultimate safety depended on an enduring control of Gibraltar and Malta.

During the Napoleonic Wars, France had been the chief enemy of India, and memories of the dramatic French invasion of Egypt lingered. France, not Russia, represented in English eyes the greater threat to the European balance of power during a decade of convalescence after the Peace. Almost inevitably, it was assumed that France would attempt to expunge the humiliations of the past by an aggressive foreign and colonial policy.

When Corsica was the only off-shore French possession, the Mediterranean had not been a military theatre of first importance; in the eighteenth century, the Atlantic and Channel ports had been pre-eminent. But in 1830, the conquest of Algiers put France astride the Mediterranean route to India; it made her primarily a Mediterranean power. (France, wrote an acute political commentator, Hyppolyte Lamarche, did not seize Algeria simply for pulse or corn.[1]) Almost immediately, Toulon succeeded Brest as the leading French seaport, and for the general public the Mediterranean began to regain some of the allure that it possessed in the days of Napoleonic adventure. Long before Napoleon III brought the phrase into colloquial currency, the old dream of a 'French Lake' was revived. With growing fleet concentrations in Toulon, it was clear that a new policy of expansion had been

---

[1] See among his earliest publications, *L'Algérie, son influence sur les destinées de la France et de l'Europe* (Paris, 1846), 55 pp. For the moment, however, the taking of Algiers, according to the Prince de Joinville, was received like any ordinary piece of news, and did nothing to tighten the bonds between country and king. The conquest was 'a proof of the national strength, of political courage and foresight', but it effected no reconciliation with the Bourbons, and the days of Charles X were numbered (*Memoirs*, trans. Mary Loyd (New York and London, 1895), pp. 33-4).

set in train, and that France was once again emerging as Britain's most formidable rival. Under the energizing direction of the son of Louis Philippe, the Prince de Joinville, the construction of a steam navy went steadily ahead.

Already in command of nearly 600 miles of north African coast-line, France relentlessly pursued influence in Tunisia and Egypt. By the end of the thirties she could count on the Egyptian Pasha's eleven ships of the line which she had helped to build and whose officers she had trained. French engineers had constructed an arsenal and a dry-dock at Alexandria, and were busily engaged in making it a fortress. The French government, as Palmerston saw it, was solidly behind Mehemet Ali's project of an independent state consisting of Syria, Egypt and Arabia. Once this was accomplished, Tunis and Tripoli would be pressed into the same system, and France would become practically mistress of the Mediterranean.[1]

British power in this sea had been exercised for much of the eighteenth century from the base at Minorca, and since the early nineteenth century from Malta. Gibraltar, as guardian of the straits, continued to be an indispensable anchorage and port of refreshment. Beyond Malta no strong naval power lay athwart the corridor, save Egypt, whose policies of expansion at the expense of the Ottoman empire France was supporting in her own interest. Strategically, the logical if politically hazardous solution for France was to extend her effective control of north African shores eastward, and acquire Egypt by influence or gradual infiltration. Thence she would be in a position to drive a salient deep into Egypt, and cut the vital Isthmus road to the East. Such an achievement, the French consul-general at Alexandria later noted with pardon-

---

[1] To Lord Granville, 10 December 1839; F.O. 27, vol. 578.

able enthusiasm would be more disastrous to Britain than if France occupied an English county.[1] In such an event, Palmerston wrote Lord Granville in 1839, '...any British government would be compelled by publick opinion to resist ...by war, if circumstances should prove ineffectual'.[2]

The alternative short of war was to stake a claim at some strategic harbour point on either side of the Isthmus, and there establish a naval base capable of nourishing a squadron. History had demonstrated how a well-placed harbour like Mauritius (Isle de France) could be the means of damaging or disrupting enemy communications. A French squadron on the south Arabian coast, for example, would be beautifully placed to contest and thwart British interests in the Red Sea and the Persian Gulf; French control of a base in Asia Minor could mean in time of war the blocking of the vulnerable Isthmus portage.

Although she would have intervened to forestall any overt French attempt, no British government seriously contemplated the occupation of Egypt before 1882. Britain preferred —sometimes with French co-operation—to bend her energies towards propping up the rickety Ottoman empire as a buffer against Russian designs on the Straits or the Euphrates valley. Admittedly, the buffer might disintegrate. British treaties with the Sublime Porte were no guarantee that either the Turkish empire or the highways to India which it flanked could be maintained intact. Indeed, Turkey's weakness, partly a consequence of Egypt's quasi-independence under Mehemet Ali, invited interventions that even British sea power could not prevent.

[1] See C. W. Hallberg, *The Suez Canal, its History and Diplomatic Importance* (New York, 1931), pp. 104–5.   [2] 10 December 1839; F.O. 27, vol. 578.

In 1832 Mehemet had defeated the main Turkish army at Konieh, swept over Syria and threatened Constantinople. The sultan appealed in vain for British naval assistance against his presumptuous vassal, but nearly a year elapsed before the Mediterranean fleet was reinforced, and during that interval a Russian squadron, in response to the sultan's appeal, had moved from the Black Sea and anchored off the Golden Horn. The reason for this otherwise inexplicable failure to assist the sultan, was, as Palmerston confessed a year later, a singularly uncomplicated one. With only fourteen line-of-battle ships in commission, and two other international crises brewing— Portugal and Holland were the critical areas—Britain was physically incapable of responding at once to the sultan's appeal.[1]

Hence, by the time Britain and France had brought hostilities to a standstill, Russia had established paramount influence over the Porte; indeed, the ambiguous Treaty of Unkiar Skelessi (8 July 1833) seemed likely to give her a right-of-way through the Bosphorus, with eventual control of the destinies of the Ottoman empire.[2] Admittedly, Mehemet Ali's feudal

---

[1] Bartlett, *Great Britain and Sea Power, 1815-1853* (Oxford, 1963), pp. 90-1. It is understandable that prolonged inquiries in regard to Russian naval strength should have been undertaken after 1832, culminating in the Admiralty's elaborate memorandum of November 1838 on the state of the Royal Navy in comparison with the estimated real and prospective strength, not only of Russia, but of France, Egypt and Turkey (Ad. 3/264).

In July 1836 the Royal Navy mustered twenty ships of the line in commission, of which six were in the Mediterranean, and throughout 1838, twenty-two, of which nine were in the Mediterranean at the beginning of that year. By 1839 the total had risen to nearly thirty, of which the Mediterranean total by July was eleven. See *Navy List, 1836-9*.

[2] The Treaty, which was intended to last for eight years, required each nation to come to the other's aid in case of attack, but the so-called secret article relieved the Turks of this obligation on the understanding that the Dardanelles should be closed to all foreign warships. The Russians withdrew from Constantinople on 10 July 1833.

71

domain straddled both the Euphrates and the Red Sea route to India; but he was no more capable of guaranteeing unrestricted passage through Egypt than was the sultan. Egypt had become, in both the military and commercial sense, the vital hinge of the British empire; yet it was now perfectly clear that its security under British auspices was anything but assured. Britain could not guarantee the corridor against an unfavourable upset of the European balance. She could not alone hope to stem the advance of an invading force driving southward through Syria.[1]

Britain had faced European coalitions during the war of American Independence, and suffered near-disaster. In the time of Napoleon she had managed to survive the mortal threat of a Continent bludgeoned into unity under a single rule. The spectre of standing alone persisted throughout the nineteenth century. Conceivably, a similar critical situation could recur, with Britain again in isolation. It could be assumed that the French would seek to achieve such an end, as much to avenge hurt pride as to exploit military opportunities. Supposing France and Russia came together in thievish partnership—France to get Egypt and possibly Syria, and Russia the control of Persia whose policies she was already shaping? Such a prospect fostered the British nightmare—a continental alliance from which she was excluded.

To avoid such a catastrophe the obvious aim was to isolate France by courting Russia, and this Palmerston was fortunate in accomplishing partly because Nicholas I personally suspected and disliked Louis Philippe, and also because he feared a *mariage de convenance* between France and Great Britain.

---

[1] Cf. R. Robinson and J. Gallagher, *Africa and the Victorians* (London, 1961), pp. 77–8.

Although a strong Black Sea fleet was stationed only four days' sail from the Bosphorus, Nicholas had gauged the consequences which would follow a sudden seizure of the Straits. While recognizing that the collapse of the sultan's government might force this action in anticipation of a French or British attempt, he also knew that such a step would almost inevitably lead to war with the rest of Europe.[1] An unsuccessful if not a disastrous war against a European coalition would not only imperil Russia's shaky and corrupt internal administration, it would certainly destroy her influence both in Turkey and Persia.[2] On the other hand, provided Russia and Britain worked together to curb Mehemet Ali and stabilize the Ottoman empire, it was unlikely that Louis Philippe would risk the use of force against a predominant coalition. In fact this was the way events worked out between 1839 and 1840, when the so-called Near Eastern crisis reached combustion point.

The drama opened early in 1837 when Mehemet Ali, with French encouragement, began moving his troops into central Arabia, whence in due course a column was directed through Mesopotamia towards Bagdad and the Persian Gulf. Another column had fanned out along the eastern coast of the Red Sea in the direction of Aden. By the end of 1837 it had reached a point some sixty miles to the southward of Mocha. Control of the two important overland highways between Europe and Asia—the Red Sea route and the Euphrates—seemed within reach of the ruler of Egypt, who might conceivably try to consolidate his gains by making a deal with Russia or

[1] See Philip E. Moseley, *Russian Diplomacy and the Opening of the Eastern Question in 1838 and 1839* (Harvard Historical Monographs (Cambridge, Mass., 1934)), pp. 6–7, 36–9.
[2] C. K. Webster, *Palmerston*, II, 751.

France. Obviously Britain could view with indifference neither the extinction of the river route to the Persian Gulf, so recently surveyed by Colonel Chesney, nor possible Franco-Egyptian control of the Isthmus, which, if Mehemet's successes continued, might very well become a private Franco-Egyptian avenue joining Alexandria to Suez. '...the gradual approach of France to India by the way of Egypt', wrote the governor of Bombay, Sir Robert Grant, 'simultaneously with that of Russia by the way of Persia, is not to be treated as an event beyond the pale of possibility....[1]'

It was fear of this development which led to the occupation of Aden at the mouth of the Red Sea, as an outpost of India's defences. British authorities at home would have preferred to buy Aden from the local sultan as part of a lawful real estate deal; but there was no time for haggling negotiations. Consequently, before Mehemet's troops reached the neighbourhood of the port, a small Bombay expedition took possession by assault in January 1839. The opposition was noisy but ineffective; British losses amounted, in killed and wounded, to about fifteen men.[2] Aden was the first base ever held in Arabia by a European power. It was occupied not as a conquest, but by lease in perpetuity from the sultan of Lahej, whose annual pension could be regarded as ground rent.

Aden did, indeed, provide a convenient coal depot adjacent to the Red Sea, and judging by the correspondence it is probable that Palmerston was influenced by the needs of

[1] (India Office) Minute of 26 March 1838; Secret Consultation no. 12, 4 April 1838; Bombay Secret Proceedings, vol. 96.

[2] For a description of the proceedings of 18 and 19 January see Rear-Admiral Sir F. L. Maitland to Charles Wood, *Wellesley* at Bombay, 20 February 1839 (no. 21) enclosing report of Captain Smith of H.M.S. *Volage*, 22 January 1839, and a report of the Political Resident, Captain T. B. Haines, 16 January 1839; Ad. 1/219.

steam communication. But the paramount, motivating reason for the acquisition was fear of European competition; and, in this sense, good harbours in the Indian Ocean, like small squadrons in the Persian Gulf, may be regarded not as inconsiderable items on the scales of the European balance. Aden offered a guarantee against French intervention and French exploitation of tribal politics in areas adjacent to the Red Sea. It was occupied partly because of its advantages as a coaling and military station, but chiefly to prevent any other power from taking it. Aden was an additional rivet of British power. The Near East needed its Malta—a base that offered good facilities for naval concentrations in force should the Red Sea route to India be endangered by competitors unfriendly to Britain.

Meanwhile, at the eastern end of the Arabian stage, three months after Aden had fallen, an Egyptian column under Khurshid Pasha had stormed its way to the Persian Gulf, and summoned the ruler of Bahrein to surrender. To some frightened observers a second Alexander was marching on India. Unfortunately for the Pasha, a narrow stretch of water separated the island from the mainland. An insignificant detachment of the Indian Navy was sufficient to bar his way, and bluff his newly subjugated tribal vassals into neutrality.

As usual, Asia's eruptions were Europe's problems; the main threats to India's security were always European in origin. Command of the sea was a European issue, and one that could not be decided in the Indian Ocean. Palmerston never really worried about his ability to cut Mehemet Ali's Arabian empire 'to size'. As the President of the Board of Control put it: 'If we come to blows with the Pasha, we shall not confine ourselves to Arabia. There is such a sea as the Mediterranean, and such a city as Alexandria.'[1] But such confident pronouncements assumed adequate naval forces in the Mediterranean, a postulate that was being steadily eroded by mounting evidence of French imperial designs. In fact fear of France became Palmerston's obsession. In 1839 he was far less disturbed by Egyptian advances to the Persian Gulf than by the bellicose renaissance of France. It was fortunate, as temperatures mounted feverishly in 1839, that he was supported by his traditional luck, his customary flair for diplomacy, and an uncharacteristic restraint.

While French agents were assailing, thwarting or gnawing at British interests in Egypt, Syria, Turkey and Greece, the Mediterranean seemed to be swarming with French steamers and battleships. At the beginning of 1840, it was assumed that France had seventeen line-of-battle ships in the Mediterranean, eleven of them cruising in Levant waters. The Turco-Egyptian fleet, the greater part in Alexandria harbour, amounted to nineteen of the line and twenty frigates. To oppose this local force of thirty battleships (because the defection of the Turkish fleet to Egypt has to be taken into account) and as many frigates and steamers, Britain had twelve of the line and half a dozen frigates.[2] Indeed, French superiority in the Mediterranean was such as to tempt an assault on Malta in the summer of 1840; and French naval officers pressed their government for permission to open fire on British ships.[3]

---

[1] John Cam Hobhouse to Sir James Carnac, 4 May 1840 (I.O., Miscel.839, p. 345).
[2] See Strength and Disposition Lists of the Royal Navy; also, State of the French Navy, according to Charles Wood's memorandum of November 1838 (Ad. 3/264), which does not, however, list dispositions.
[3] Auckland to Russell, 30 August 1848 (Russell Papers, P.R.O. 30/22/7).

That Paris demurred was not through any fear of British naval power;[1] Louis Philippe drew back before the prospect of a continental combination. In July both Austria and Russia declared their intention of maintaining the integrity of the Ottoman empire.[2] In November, Admiral Stopford's 'whiff of grape shot' was sufficient to subdue the forts of Acre, thus smashing beyond repair the Pasha's great design of an Arab kingdom stretching from the Nile to the Euphrates.[3] By December, as a result of conventions concluded at Alexandria, Mehemet surrendered Crete, Syria and Arabia, and in renouncing Arabia, he abandoned Khurshid Pasha's conquests, represented by a score of desert outposts that straggled towards the Persian Gulf.

In retrospect it is clear that despite the obvious weakness of the East Indies squadron, British control of the Persian Gulf and Arabian Sea was never in question. British naval resources in Persian and Arabian waters were sufficient for the purpose of limited blockade until a decision was reached in the west. As long as a British squadron with available allied support could command the Mediterranean, large-scale landings were possible, for example, anywhere on the coast of Syria. Control of the Mediterranean enabled Great Britain to exercise enormous military leverage. The mobility provided by secure communications permitted the use of a fleet with hardly less effect than that obtained by the presence of a large army. Not only were the peninsulas that became Italy

---

[1] See Admiral Bowles to Lord Haddington, 22 September 1844 (Appx. Q to the Report from the Select Committee on Navy, Army and Ordnance Estimates, 1847–1848, vol. XXI, pt. 2, pp. 1110–12).

[2] Palmerston was also able to include Austria and Prussia in the partnership.

[3] Harold Temperley, *England and the Near East: The Crimea* (London, 1936), pp. 126–30; for a discussion of naval proceedings during the campaign of 1839–40 see R. C. Anderson, *Naval Wars in the Levant*, pp. 552–66.

and Greece open to her intervention, even Russian bases on the Black Sea were vulnerable, provided an acquiescent Sultan opened the Straits.

But, again, one must emphasize the words 'available allied support'. The favourable decision in 1840 which paved the way for a new international agreement in the Straits in 1841[1] was based principally on the isolation of France. Palmerston's diplomacy which aimed at safeguarding the route to India against two jealous and powerful rivals was not buttressed in the Mediterranean by an over-all supremacy in ships. Britain was not in a position to safeguard her Mediterranean interests single-handed. Hence the reluctance of Lord Palmerston (like Lord Rosebery in a similar situation half a century later),[2] to 'get tough' with France is not difficult to understand. The British government and the Admiralty were acutely aware of their inability to cope with the Toulon fleet. In the event of a Franco-British war, France might well, as Palmerston was to argue ten years later, sweep up British commerce, seize the Isthmus and advance on India long before 'our reinforcements, naval and military, could arrive by long sea voyage'.[3] Had the French attempted to make use of their superior force in the Mediterranean in 1839, Palmerston would have been compelled, as he confessed, to call in 'ten Russian sail of the line'.[4] He was saved from this embarrass-

---

[1] The agreement indirectly cancelled the Treaty of Unkiar Skelessi of July 1833 by closing the Straits, while Turkey was at peace, to the warships of all nations.

[2] See Arthur Marsden, 'Britain and the "Tunis Base", 1894–1899', *English Historical Review*, LXXIX, no. cccx (January 1964), 70.

[3] This fearful conjecture is based on Palmerston's testimony of 1860 wherein he described the French project of a canal as conceived 'in hostility to the interests and policy of England'. Cited by H. C. F. Bell, *Lord Palmerston* (London, 1936), II, 357.

[4] C. J. Bartlett, *Great Britain and Sea Power, 1815–1853*, p. 132.

ment by the Quadruple Coalition (negotiated in July 1840) which forced France to back down.

Obviously, then, the security of British overland routes did not depend on a constant British supremacy in the Mediterranean. Britain could only aim at an indisputable command of the Channel and Atlantic waters with ready access to the Strait of Gibraltar.[1] In this respect, paradoxical as it may appear, the southward expansion of the French empire was subsequently regarded by the Admiralty as a strategic convenience. The vulnerability of the north African coast tended to reduce any potential threat from French ports in the English Channel. Colonies in the Mediterranean pinned down a substantial proportion of French naval strength. The further that French dominion in north Africa was extended, the greater the naval dispositions to defend it. In a sense, Algeria and subsequent acquisitions could be considered as useful hostages of the Royal Navy.

When France occupied Tunis in April 1881, although the Foreign Office was somewhat agitated by the threat to Malta, 240 miles to the south-east, the Admiralty was unconcerned.[2] Even when France some ten years later prepared to build a 'second Toulon' at Bizerta, commanding the narrowest part of the inland sea, the Admiralty showed no lack of confidence in their ability to crush the French fleet should public excite-

---

[1] In December, 1839, owing to the Near East crisis, and other emergency commitments the force in home waters was momentarily reduced to eight brigs. Twelve line-of-battle ships were in the Mediterranean; three in the Tagus and three with the East Indies squadron—a dissipation of strength which was partly the consequence of the Palmerston gambling instinct. See Bartlett, *op. cit.* pp. 135-7.

[2] The First Lord, the Earl of Northbrook, made this quite clear to Lord Granville; see communications of 19 April and 13 May, quoted in W. N. Medlicott, *Bismarck, Gladstone and the Concert of Europe* (London, 1956), p. 310.

ment lead to war.[1] 'Biserta clutches the Mediterranean by the throat', wrote Gabriel Hanotaux.[2] Although such fiery pretensions were fashionable at the time in French official circles, the British government was not unduly alarmed to see a rival squander her substance in such 'misdirected efforts'. In Lord Salisbury's view the dissipation of public funds on fixed installations rather than warships would weaken France, besides contributing to the further dispersion of her fleet.[3]

This attitude of official tranquillity, however smugly or sincerely held, was not based, as has been said, on any implicit assumption of over-all naval superiority. It owed its origins partly to the general disinclination of European powers after 1815 to risk their stability and their well-being in further expensive wars, and partly to the British capacity to gather allies against any aggressor who would upset the *status quo*. For good and selfish political reasons Britain was the power that consistently opposed change in the interest of continental stability. Britain aimed at being the 'mediator' or 'balancer', and she could perform this function effectively simply because the differences among the other powers were greater than their collective differences with herself.[4] In the pursuit of this essenti-

[1] A. J. Marder, *The Anatomy of British Sea Power* (New York, 1940), p. 219; published in London in 1941 as *British Naval Policy, 1880–1905*, p. 219. British naval strength at this time barely exceeded that of France and Russia in alliance, and the combined building estimates for 1893 were substantially greater than those of Britain (W. L. Langer, *Diplomacy of Imperialism* (2nd ed., New York, 1951), p. 46; Marder, *op. cit.* pp. 162–3).

[2] *La Paix Latine* (Paris, 1903), p. 276; quoted in Marsden, *op. cit.* p. 79.

[3] Count Hatzfeldt's report of a conversation with Lord Salisbury in June 1896; see Marsden, *op. cit.* p. 81.

[4] H. A. Kissinger, *A World Restored: Metternich, Castlereagh and the Problems of Peace 1812–22* (Cambridge, Mass., 1957), p. 31. In this connection, note E. V. Gulick's thoughtful study, *Europe's Classical Balance of Power* (Cornell University Press, 1955), especially chapters II and XIII.

ally defensive policy the navy was merely the indispensable adjunct of the diplomacy; it provided the cutting edge.

In the beginning, the ends of British policy required the isolation of France, but after the debacle of 1832-3, when Russia occupied Constantinople, the old equilibrium of 1815 had to be readjusted; and as new problems arose and new threats appeared, the process of adjustment became almost continuous—to meet the challenge of France in 1840, Russia in 1854-8, and again Russia between 1878 and 1879.

For a moment the Crimean War seemed to have justified itself by terminating for the time being Russian aggression in the direction of the Straits. By the Treaty of Paris, Britain, Austria and France imposed on Russia a settlement that included the neutralization of the Black Sea. But the ink of official obligation was hardly dry before Napoleon III became involved in the movement for Italian freedom. Both he and Cavour were anxious to bury the hatchet in order to buy Russian support against Austria. In July 1858 a Russian squadron left Kronstadt for the Mediterranean, and not long afterwards it was announced that Russia had been granted port facilities in the harbour of Villafranca, two miles from Nice. This 'small Sebastopol', so described by an English journalist, offered 'as good a footing as even Constantinople for future operations in Syria, Greece, and the Levant'. 'For more than a hundred years', said the *Morning Chronicle* of 11 September 1858, 'the chief object of Russian ambition has been to obtain a naval *point d'appui* in the Mediterranean'. That object 'so long desired and so strenuously resisted' had at last been accomplished.[1]

Happily for a nervous Admiralty and a boiling public this

---

[1] Quoted in W. E. Mosse, *The Rise and Fall of the Crimean System, 1855–71* (London, 1963), pp. 112–13.

spectacular challenge to the British policy of the *status quo* was short-lived. Although a few Russian ships continued to use the port (which was given to France in 1860) the demand for internal reforms and budgetary economies was stronger than the passion for distant adventure; and after 1870 when Russia repudiated the Black Sea clauses the project of a Mediterranean naval base lost most of its strategic validity.[1] Not until 1893—the year of the famous Naval Scare—did the Russian government, at the invitation of France, re-establish a small squadron at Villefranche (Villafranca), with the right to use Toulon for refitment and repair.[2]

So the Dardanelles remained the crucial point of contact for British and Russian policies. As Messrs Robinson and Gallagher have observed, the main line of defence against Russia continued to be the Turkish empire in Asia, with its pivot resting upon Constantinople.[3] Only narrow straits separated the main naval strength of Russia from British ships which sought to secure the gateway to the Red Sea. But as long as Britain was in a position to bar the Black Sea outlet to the Mediterranean, she could use her fleets to bolster the sultan's empire against Russian influence, or to repel in moments of crisis the grandiose designs of rebellious parvenus like Mehemet Ali. Events had demonstrated her ability, with the help of allies, to accomplish these objectives. For this reason, as most Russain statesmen recognized after 1860, the Black Sea route to the Dardanelles could never be Russia's line of least resistance—rather the contrary. British sensitivity

---

[1] Mosse, *op. cit.* p. 125.

[2] Marder, *op. cit.* pp. 175, 178–9 n., 182. The new Russian squadron consisted of a second-class battleship and three cruisers; the Black Sea fleet was based on four new fast battleships, of which three were first-class.

[3] Robinson and Gallagher, *Africa and the Victorians*, p. 82.

to any threat to the Suez–Red Sea route had been manifest long before the Crimean War, and if anything it grew in acuteness. The loss of the Cape would have been regarded as a damaging blow: the permanent occupation of the Straits by Russia, even before the Suez Canal was cut, as a catastrophe.[1]

It must be recognized, however, that Britain was never completely dependent on the overland routes to preserve her links with India. The Cape route was still the major commercial, and until 1869 the major military, tie with India. Nonetheless, the danger to the security of India inherent in the occupation of the Red Sea littoral or the Euphrates valley by a great European power continued, as I have previously emphasized, to haunt British statesmen ever since Napoleon had struck out for the East in 1798.

Before the thirties, Admiralty strategy had never been affected by the possibility of a Russian squadron operating against India from ports in the Persian Gulf. In retrospect, such a proposition appears as absurd as the Duke of Wellington's curious judgment that the Russian Baltic fleet was in a position to land 30,000 men in India. Beginning with the thirties, however, strategic geography 'went out the window' as politicians and journalists morbidly contemplated the Eurasian giant permanently camped on the Persian Gulf, or wading confidently across the Indus. Indeed, many soldiers and sailors believed that Russia's main hope of neutralizing British naval power lay in progressive expansion by land in areas where campaigns would not suffer unduly from bad communications.

The first seeds of suspicion had taken root in 1826 when a boundary dispute between Russia and Persia culminated in

---

[1] Cf. A. T. Mahan, *The Problem of Asia and its effect upon International Policies* (Boston, 1900), p. 117.

two years of bitter war and the cession by Persia of two trans-Caucasian provinces. Suspicion turned to acute anxiety following the treaty of Unkiar Skelessi which seemed in British eyes to confirm Russia's determination to break into the open sea. The crises of 1839–40, by bringing London and Moscow into the same camp, merely served to blanket the fearful spectre of Russian imperialism. '...if Englishmen had no connection with India except by the Cape,' wrote C. W. Crawley, 'they would have cared a great deal less about Russian doings in the Balkans.'[1] Lord Salisbury's observation of 1889 is equally relevant:'Were it not for possessing India, we should trouble ourselves but little about Persia.'[2]

For 'Persia' one may also read 'Persian Gulf'. If, for example, Russia were to decide on an advance southwards to the Euphrates, and thence to the Persian Gulf, British sea power could do nothing to retard her progress unless, with Turkish consent, the British squadron was allowed to create a diversion by entering the Black Sea. And, if Russia were able to establish a fortified port near the mouth of the Shatt-el-Arab, she could not only block the Tigris-Euphrates route; theoretically she might win control of the Persian Gulf, and be in a position to outflank the Red Sea route to India—indeed, all the main routes leading to the East. Such action could conceivably alter the whole strategic balance in the Indian Ocean, and involve a drastic reorganization of British naval resources in eastern waters. At the least, a Russian base in the Gulf would have distractionary and nuisance value. A few Russian warships, along with those of conscribed Arab satel-

[1] 'Anglo-Russian Relations, 1815–1840', *Cambridge Historical Journal*, III, no. 1 (1929), 69.
[2] India Office to Foreign Office, 22 May 1889 (F.O. 60/506; quoted Rose L. Greaves, *Persia and the Defence of India, 1884–1892* (London, 1959), p. 25).

lites, could temporarily complicate the British position in an ocean where local command had hitherto been safely preserved by a ship of the line and half a dozen sloops and frigates.

Whether a descent towards the Gulf was ever considered by Moscow is most improbable. Yet statesmen of the day, and soldiers too, were not driven willy-nilly by public and press hysteria. They had seen the vanguard of Russian armies push down from the Caucasus in 1828; they saw the Caspian turned into a Russian lake, and their agents spied Russian scouts filtering into the valleys and defiles of the north-west frontier. Fear bred suspicion, and gave wings to imagination. Menacing flourishes in the general direction of India's north-west frontier might well be masking Russia's real plan of campaign, namely, an advance down the Tigris–Euphrates valley with the object of winning a permanent naval and commercial base on the Persian Gulf.

The government were concerned about their Asian flank, but there was little preventive action they could take, apart from examining the state of existing communications through the medium of select committees.[1] In 1832 detailed evidence was sought not only on the success of Bombay's experiments with a steam route to the Red Sea, but in regard to further exploration of the Euphrates system as an alternative water-way to India.[2] Since the evidence available seemed incon-

---

[1] In January 1832, under the chairmanship of the President of the Board of Control, Charles Grant, one such committee was appointed to investigate 'the present state of the Affairs of the East India Company, and to inquire into the State of Trade between Great Britain, the East Indies and China' (*Parl. Papers*, 1831–2, VIII, p. 2).

[2] See T. B. Macaulay (India Board) to Barrow (Secretary of Admiralty), 5 February 1833, enclosing a report by the 'friends of the steam route', with plans and estimates, 14 March 1832 (Ad. 1/3920). Evidence received by the committee is contained in *Parl. Papers*, 1831–2, X, pt. 2, pp. 675–766.

clusive, no recommendations were made to Parliament, but a second investigating committee appointed in 1834 felt less inhibited. By that time the S.S. *Hugh Lindsay* had made five voyages between Bombay and Aden, and shown the practicality of the Red Sea route during at least eight months of the year.

On the other hand, the committee of 1834 felt that the alternative route—from Alexandretta on the Syrian coast, overland to the Euphrates and down the river to the Gulf—should at least be tried.[1] Although river navigation would be difficult during the dry season when reefs and sandbanks rose above low water, an inland waterway was safe from the worst extremes of sea weather. Moreover, the low-water season in Mesopotamia—November to February—did not coincide with one troublesome monsoon period—June to September; hence, the two routes might conceivably be synchronized by alternating Mediterranean schedules according to the season.[2]

In fact, strategic considerations were far more compulsive than technical or commercial in directing the committee towards a compromise recommendation. The implications of the Treaty of Unkiar Skelessi had deeply stirred both public and government, and political expediency dictated an experiment that was certainly dubious as a commercial and military venture. Some sort of action was required to preserve order among restless tribes, and to keep Russia away from a corridor that ran from Syria through Bagdad to the Persian Gulf. If

[1] See Captain F. R. Chesney, *Reports on the Navigation of the Euphrates submitted to the Government* (London, 1833). Also his evidence before the Select Committee on Steam Navigation to India (*Parl. Papers*, 1834, XIV, pp. 20–33).

[2] Report from Select Committee on Steam Navigation to India (*Parl. Papers*, 1834, XIV, p. 11; *Hansard*, 3rd series, XXV, 930–2; also Hoskins, *British Routes to India*, pp. 158–9).

she won control of the upper reaches of the Tigris, Russia might at the proper season float any number of troops and supplies as far as Basra, whence her forces could strike south-ward to the sea or into the heart of Persia.[1] A steam river line would, it was hoped, help to counteract such a project by giving Britain an obvious vested interest. '...all our political interest, in the way of guarding against Russia, lies in the Persian Gulf, and not at all in the Red Sea, where we have no business, political or commercial of any importance whatever....'.[2]

Although Colonel Chesney's steam trials between 1835 and 1836 confirmed the inadequacy of the Euphrates as a water route, Palmerston was determined that a right-of-way should be maintained to discourage any Russian attempt at trespass. A well-used and supervised boundary thoroughfare might be the means of avoiding further painful and risky diplomatic contests in Persia, and of bolstering the sultan against the ravages of his ambitious feudatory, Mehemet Ali.[3] So work on the river route must go on. The landward claim had already been staked by dromedary post along a line that ran from Bagdad to Damascus and Beirut, whence steamers from Alexandria could make the necessary connections.[4] On the main river course officers of the Indian Navy continued their surveys above Basra; and even when the main task was completed in 1842, a small armed steamer was left behind to protect British interests at Bagdad, and to continue the

---

[1] Arthur Conolly, *Journey to the North of India, Overland from England, through Russia, Persia and Affghaunistaun* (London, 1834); and Lieutenant Alexander Burnes, *Travels into Bokhara* (London, 1834); reviewed in *Quarterly Review*, LII (1834), 57, 405.

[2] Evidence of Thomas Love Peacock before the Select Committee on Steam Navigation to India (*Parl. Papers*, 1834, XIV, p. 11).

[3] See Crawley, 'Anglo-Russian Relations, 1815-1840', *op. cit.* p. 70.

[4] See G. R. Porter, *The Progress of the Nation* (1838 ed.), p. 51; (1851 ed.), p. 320.

exploration of the swampy maze between the Tigris and Euphrates rivers. Indeed, not until the Indian Navy was dissolved in 1863 did the company cease to appoint a 'Surveyor of Mesopotamia'.[1]

Actually no real threat to the Mesopotamia corridor developed until the end of the century when *Drang nach Osten* became a slogan of German industrial imperialism. What mattered to Russia was not the Persian Gulf *per se*; what counted was the leverage she was able to exert, especially in times of emergency, on the policies and practices of the Persian government. In 1841, only two and a half years after the British occupation of the island of Kharak (close to the Persian shore near Bushire), Russian pressures on the Persian government were sufficient to force a military withdrawal. Following the British retreat from Afghanistan in 1842—until 1942 the worst defeat in the history of the British army in the East—even the coal depot on the island had to be abandoned. Because Russian influence in the Persian Court was supreme, the Shah was literally blackmailed into acquiescence.

Yet the Russian government, as distinct from its exuberant agents or indiscreet plenipotentiaries, was never seriously attracted by dreams of Indian conquest. The very considerable obstacles of geography facing any invading force approaching by way of Persia presented problems of logistics that were then insoluble. Even if the Russians had succeeded in controlling the Shatt-el-Arab, they would have been hard put to make use of it. Basra was almost a thousand miles from the Indus; there were no natural harbours at the northern end of the Gulf; the climate was insufferable and the adjoining countryside was bleak and sterile. So long as Britain con-

[1] Hoskins, *op. cit.* p. 182.

trolled the Arabian Sea, even a riverside dockyard would have been a gamble. Indeed, any kind of fortified base would have been neutralized by the British navy. Russian command of the Gulf was simply out of the question. The Honourable gentlemen in Whitehall and Downing Street, remarked Joseph Hume, in a glib judgment that happened to be sound, 'had talked so much about Russia, that they were afraid of a monster they had created'.[1]

On the other hand, it was reasonable to conclude that Russia would never be satisfied with her limited and politically circumscribed connections to the oceans of the world through the Baltic and the Black Sea. In terms of maritime commerce as well as military strategy, it was obviously in the Russian interest to acquire by possession or influence unenclosed ports that could not, at a moment's notice, be shut against her by a hostile power.[2] Consequently, just as Britain underpinned and buttressed Turkey in the interests of Straits' security, so was the territorial integrity of Persia and the security of the Gulf accepted as a strategic necessity. The inland sea that marked the eastern boundary of the Arab world was part of the maritime frontier of India. Any relaxation of British control in the Persian Gulf, whether by formal concession to Persia, or by neglect of Russian military infiltration into Persia or Mesopotamia, might imperil not only an overland route to India, but the political stability of India itself.

---

[1] Debate of 4 March 1836; Committee of Supply—Naval Estimates (Hansard, 3rd series, XXXI, pp. 1235–6).

[2] The chief exponent of the Persian Gulf thesis at the beginning of the nineteenth century was John Malcolm, subsequently governor of Bombay, whose visions of a Russian doorway on the Indian Ocean were described in a series of reports and warnings from the time of his first mission.

In the nineteenth century, British policy followed at least three consistent courses: one, upholding the independence of the Low Countries against the intrusion of any great power; two, keeping an adequate naval superiority; and three, maintaining the Indian empire, which meant, in consequence, safeguarding two overland lines of communication—the short passage across the Isthmus of Suez to the Red Sea, and the less convenient river route down the Euphrates valley to the Persian Gulf. Neither Gibraltar, Malta, Aden or the Cape, for all their importance, held quite the same significance as the less tractable and less accessible territories of the Ottoman empire which contained these highways to the East. The opening of de Lesseps Canal in 1869, theoretically under the auspices of an international corporation, served only to augment rather than diminish the operation and influence of British diplomacy in the Near East. In July 1882, when a French squadron refused to help Admiral Seymour shell the fortifications of Alexandria and bring Arabi's nationalists to terms, Egypt became for all intents and purposes a British protectorate.[1]

Throughout the eastern crisis of 1876–8, Gladstone had strongly condemned any plans to take over Egypt, just as

[1] By the Suez Canal Convention of 1888 the Canal was not neutralized, but internationalized as a 'free and open' waterway; it remained an extraterritorial adjunct of Egypt, nominally within the sovereignty of the sultan of Turkey, but strategically within the power of the keeper of the Mediterranean gateway, Great Britain.

The Convention was signed on 29 October 1888 by the representatives of France, Germany, Austria-Hungary, Italy, Russia, Spain, Turkey, the Netherlands, and Great Britain. But Britain did not formally adhere to the convention until the Anglo-French agreement of April 1904 was signed, and then only on condition that the articles guaranteeing the right of way to all nations in time of war, and the repudiation of blockade, should remain in abeyance.

Although the Protectorate existed in law only from 1914 to 1922, Egyptian allegiance to Turkey after the British occupation in 1882 was only nominal.

Palmerston from the forties to the sixties had systematically opposed the construction of the Suez Canal. Britain had no wish to defend a Canal or to occupy either Egypt or Syria. She aimed at keeping the Ottoman empire alive and kicking to prevent both Russia and France from muscling in. Disraeli's rejection of Bismarck's hints that Egypt might be acquired by a *coup de main* was based on standard doctrine. Although Gladstone had sought the approval of other powers in 1882, he was *not* trying to whitewash an intervention which he resented, regretted and swore to be only temporary.[1] None the less, his action broke the spell represented by the *status quo*. By occupying Egypt, Britain had upset a balance which she herself had for more than half a century done her best to preserve. The result of this was twenty years of conflict with France, and the dismal prospect of isolation, which, by the end of the century, had become a grim reality.

The British occupation of Egypt ensured *de facto* domination of the Suez Canal, but it in no way diminished the vulnerability of the Euphrates valley route to the Persian Gulf, hitherto subject to the variable pressures of Russian expansion in Asia. Yet, apart from political obstacles, it was never more than a second class road to India. After Basra, navigation was

---

[1] In August 1877 Gladstone had written in the *Nineteenth Century*: 'Suppose the very worst. The Canal is stopped. And what then?...It seems to be forgotten by many that there is a route to India round the Cape of Good Hope.' His views on the Egyptian question are discussed in Medlicott, *Bismarck, Gladstone, and the Concert of Europe*, pp. 32 ff. See also, Robinson and Gallagher, 'The Partition of Africa', *The New Cambridge Modern History, 1870–1898* (Cambridge, 1962), XI, 567–602.

Salisbury negotiated for a British withdrawal in 1887, but the Turks foolishly refused to commit themselves, still counting on their ability to play off the powers one against another. In the same year, however, Salisbury negotiated 'Agreements' with Austria and Italy to maintain the *status quo* in lands bordering on the Mediterranean. The arrangements were directed principally against the Russians and the Turks, and lasted until 1896.

less complicated, but Basra was still a long way from Bombay. None the less, British policy had been continuously directed towards safeguarding this route by maintaining naval supremacy in the Persian Gulf. The arrest of any Russian advance southwards across the line of communications to the Gulf was as consistent a British objective as the protection of the Straits.

The Russian spectre did not forsake the Euphrates valley in the later years of the nineteenth century. Indeed, it had grown ominously larger during the Russo-Turkish war of 1877–8, and only began to shrink in the face of a new and slowly recognized threat from the West. By the eighties German commercial enterprise found the field clear for an invasion of the Near East as well as Africa, and German political ambitions took the place of Russian as potential threats to the security of the last overland route to India. In 1892, with the extension of the European railway line from Constantinople to Ankara, the first step on the road to Bagdad and Basra had been taken.[1]

Just as the coming of the steamship and the submarine cable affected the direction and conduct of naval operations, so did the development of the railway accelerate the speed of military operations on land.[2] The railway became in fact the basic instrument of strategic mobility. The use or denial of railways could now determine major military objectives, and one of the main reasons for the British occupation of Cyprus in 1878 was its proximity to Alexandretta, whence a rail connection might be established through Syria to Bagdad. It was obvious that a railway system to the Persian Gulf would be a far more stable and less vulnerable line of communication than the

[1] E. M. Earle, *Turkey, the Great Powers and the Bagdad Railway* (New York, 1924), pp. 29–32; for German economic interests in the Near East, see pp. 45–52.
[2] See chap. I, p. 28, fn. 1.

seasonally erratic inland waterway. Four years later, however, when Alexandria became available, such a move seemed
less necessary; on the other hand, the rejection of the project
left the way open for a similar grand undertaking by Germany, with ominous prospects for British interests in the Near
East. The new line would outflank the Suez–Red Sea route,
and serve to nourish Turkish strength and ambitions, as some
German strategists saw it, at the expense of the British position
in Egypt.[1] It would, moreover, pose quite as serious a threat
to Russian as to British imperial designs; indeed Russian
objections in 1899 were responsible for the diversion of the
route southward from Konieh to Bagdad, via Mosul,[2] and
indirectly for Russia's willingness to sign the Anglo-Russian
agreement of 1907.

As it happened the *Bagdadbahn* was never quite completed.[3]
None the less, an unfinished railway whose iron tentacles
stretched towards the sheikdoms of the Persian Gulf was a
sufficient threat to the security of India and British oil interests
in Arabia to incite if not justify military intervention in
Mesopotamia during the First World War. By the end of
1918 the Ottoman empire was no more. Already deprived of
her north African and Balkan estates, Turkey now lost her
Arab empire, and, in effect, surrendered her titular role as
guardian of the gateway to the East.

---

[1] See Paul Rohrbach, *Die Bagdadbahn* (Berlin, 1911), pp. 18–19.

[2] Earle, *op. cit.* pp. 34–5.

[3] Originally intended to run from Constantinople to Koweit (Grane) on the
Persian Gulf, the terminus was finally after prolonged negotiations fixed at
Basra in June 1914. It was a paper agreement that was never ratified. The outbreak of war not only destroyed the agreement, it prevented the completion of
two mountain sections leading to Bagdad. None the less, '...had the Bagdad
railway been non-existent, it is doubtful if any military operations at all could
have been conducted in those regions' (Earle, *op. cit.* pp. 288–9).

More than a hundred years earlier, Napoleon had set off the train of events that culminated in the final, if momentary, clenching of British contol over the Isthmus. He had hoped to breach, if not demolish, Britain's eastern empire by occupying Egypt; and it was this danger that had first directed serious British attention to the vital importance of the short road to India. But before the thirties were out, the main threat to these communications had been transferred from France to Russia,[1] and the apparent revival of the dreams of Peter and Catherine was responsible for a succession of Near East crises that had brought British warships to the Straits, British diplomats to Constantinople in support of the crumbling sultanate, and British agents, explorers, journalists and soldiers to Persia, Afghanistan and the exotic khanates of Central Asia. Then, towards the end of the seventies, a gradual shift in the European balance transferred the threat for a third time. Before the close of the century Germany had taken the place of Russia as patron and benefactor of the Ottoman empire, and leading competitor for eastern approaches.[2]

[1] Essentially, it was a transfer of weight rather than of policy. French harassments continued, and ended only after Fashoda with the *entente* of 1904.

[2] On 15 June 1877 Lord Salisbury wrote to Lord Lytton: 'On your view that Turkey is still sustainable and that Russia is the real danger of the future, the old Crimean policy should have been clearly avowed and followed from the first. The view which, after two years' study of the subject, commends itself as the true one to my mind differs from this. The Russian power appears to me feeble, and I do not think any protection could have set the Turk upon his legs again.'

In reference to Sir Henry Rawlinson's remarks that the government were determined to keep on friendly terms with Russia because they considered Germany 'as by far the most dangerous foe to England', Salisbury wrote Lytton on 4 September 1877: 'It is obvious that in the temper of the two peoples [British and Russian], and the bitter hatred which has grown up on each side during the last twenty or thirty years, there is an obstacle to an alliance which would be fatal, even if it were likely on other grounds that Russia would care to quarrel with Germany. I am inclined to agree with the estimate Sir Henry entertains, or reports, of the relative importance to us of danger from Russia and from Ger-

The Mediterranean Corridor: Gibraltar to Bombay

For a hundred years, London, Paris, Moscow and Berlin had together or alternately sought for their own ends to preserve the independence of the Ottoman empire. But, by the end of the 1914 war, that empire was allowed to disintegrate; the prolonged process of artificial respiration was over. New kingdoms and emirates, mandates and protectorates rose from the ashes of imperial *pashaliks*, to flourish under the indulgent care of a new foreign dynasty—the grand imperial oil padishas. Turkey had lost her place of international eminence at the tri-continental cross-roads between East and West. Yet her crucial position had rarely been more than symbolic. Real authority throughout the greater part of the nineteenth century had rested in Britain, founded on a European equilibrium that enabled the Royal Navy to control the main gateways of the Mediterranean corridor— Gibraltar, the Dandanelles and Suez, as well as the great vestibule of the Euphrates valley that led to the Persian Gulf.

many...' (Lady Gwendolen Cecil, *Life of Robert, Marquis of Salisbury*, II (London, 1921), pp. 145, 150–1).

The agitated talk in press and parliament about the Russian threat to the Suez Canal when the Russo-Turkish war began in 1877 was partly owing to the fact that the Canal had only been in operation for seven years, and the problem of its defence was being thought out for the first time. In the manner of the 1830's, pamphleteers envisaged companies of Russian sappers descending on the sandy banks and blocking the passage for months at a time, on the assumption no doubt that the Russians could transport troops overland from the Caucasus faster than Britain could reinforce the vital area from Malta. Salisbury's remark, in reference to the invasion of India, about the danger of using small-scale maps, was equally appropriate to Egypt.

It should be understood too, that during the greater part of the second half of the nineteenth century Russia was quite as fearful of British ambitions as was Britain of Russia's. Many Russian diplomats and strategists including Peter Shuvalov, the ambassador in London (1877–8), believed that a Russian invasion of Turkey would be followed by a British occupation of the Straits and Constantinople, whence with superior strength she would be able to attack the south Russian coast. I am indebted to Professor Medlicott for drawing my attention to this significant point.

CHAPTER IV

THE ILLUSION OF 'PAX BRITANNICA'

By the end of the Napoleonic Wars the world position of Britain was unchallenged and almost unassailable. As a consequence of winning an over-all naval supremacy she had attained a political and military predominance that no country had hitherto reached or is ever again likely to reach. Yet apart from India the empire of 1815 was not particularly impressive except in aggregate. It was a *pot-pourri* of very varied ingredients—a timber colony in Canada, a penal colony in Australia, and an insoluble mixture of Dutch and Bantu on the peninsula of the Cape. The sugar colonies of the Caribbean were on the wane, and the great days of Indian riches were yet to come. New Zealand, still outside the imperial domain, was the casual resort of sealers and whalers, and both coasts of Africa offered as yet only pin-point openings to a dim, if not dark interior.

For a European power it represented, none the less, a well-balanced empire. Island bases and mainland trading stations were dotted in every sea, and they were tied together commercially and strategically by communication routes that led to the English Channel and the British Isles. Only a powerful fleet could sever these connections, and during the next decades no rival force was strong enough to do this; no continental nation had equal means to transport rapidly and in quantity, the arms and men necessary to contest the British overseas hegemony.

This was the firm conviction of a distinguished French

statistician, Baron Charles Dupin, who made an extremely thorough inquest of French failure in terms of British success. During four years, beginning in 1816, he travelled throughout England, investigating the sinews and sources of commercial, military and naval power. The results of his researches were published in six volumes between 1820 and 1824, and one volume was devoted to the organization of the Royal Navy. In clear, authoritative prose, which portrayed that service as an example to his countrymen, Dupin developed the argument that an immense and scattered empire which could be the weakness and ruin of any other nation was an invulnerable treasure house to its possessors simply because they controlled the sea.[1] 'It is because England is separated from her exterior provinces by enormous distances that she is not vulnerable through them; it is because these provinces are separated one from another by distances so great that they cannot at the same time fall under the blows of one adversary. To attack them is difficult; to blockade them is impossible. To supply the wants of industry, of trade, and of government, between the mother-country, and possessions scattered upon the shores of every sea, a vast number of ships is necessary, even in time of peace; and these ships ready to set sail at a moment's notice towards the threatened point, carry

---

[1] *Voyages dans La Grande-Bretagne, entrepris relativement aux services publics de la Guerre, de la Marine, et des Ponts et Chaussées, en 1816, 1817, 1818, 1819, 1820.* III. Deuxième Partie, *Force Navale de La Grande-Bretagne*, Tome premier. Constitution de la Marine (Paris, 1821); see also review in *Quarterly Review*, XXVI (1822), 25–6. Pierre Charles François Dupin (1784–1873) was a mathematician whose work in geometry led to his election to the Academy of Sciences in 1818. His *Voyages* put him into the front rank of French statisticians, and Charles X made him a baron in 1825. His great scholarly talent was, however, diluted by political activities, first in the Chamber of Deputies, and for a brief period in 1834 as a member of the Ministry of Marine where, according to the Prince de Joinville, his speeches had a marked soporific effect.

thither reinforcements and succour, which render it impregnable, either by famine or by force'.[1]

Moreover, Dupin continued, the world's trade now pivoted on London, which had become the metropolis of a national workshop. 'Thus, from one centre, by the vigour of its institutions, and the advanced state of its civil and military arts, an island which, in the Oceanic Archipelago, would scarcely be ranked in the third class, makes the effects of its industry and the weight of its power to be felt in every extremity of the four divisions of the globe....'[2]

Few would deny that Dupin, in drawing attention to Britain's dominant industrial position, was putting his finger on the outstanding feature of nineteenth-century domestic history: even as the expansion of trade after 1815 was to be the most striking feature of British maritime history—a colossal 'bursting-forth' that has never been set down in proportion.[3] While France and her subject allies on the Continent had been cut off from the outside world, Britain had been safe from invasion, and during a long period, which saw the impoverishment of a great part of Europe, she had developed new technical skills and the industrial and financial strength to exploit new markets.[4] In becoming the arsenal and paymaster of Napoleon's enemies, she had gained far more than victories in the field. She had become the leading, if not the only creditor nation. London had replaced Amster-

[1] C. Dupin, *The Commercial Power of Great Britain* (2 vols., London, 1825; originally published in Paris, 1821), vol. I, Introd. p. vi.

[2] *Ibid.* pp. v–vi.

[3] See Gerald S. Graham, *Peculiar Interlude: the Expansion of England in a Period of Peace, 1815–1850* (The Fourth George Arnold Wood Memorial Lecture (Sydney, 1959), which provided a foundation for this lecture).

[4] See H. J. Habakkuk, *American and British Technology in the Nineteenth Century* (Cambridge, 1962), pp. 185–6.

dam as the central money market of the world, and British business men and bankers, flushed with a sense of destiny, saw the universe as an oyster awaiting their prying energies, their capital and their talents.[1] On the basis of cotton, coal and iron, an expanding merchant marine and her ability to extend long-term credits, Britain was on the way to making the several quarters of the world her 'willing tributaries'.[2]

During the war years, as a consequence of the enforced isolation of the Spanish American colonies, British trade with Latin America had been enormously accelerated, and the very rapidity with which this largely illicit commerce developed ultimately committed British governments to the cause of colonial independence. By the end of the Napoleonic war, naval supremacy was so complete that Britain was not only able to assure the liberation of these Spanish and Portuguese territories, but to achieve an economic foothold and influence on both coasts of South America that no other nation could approach.[3] In the eastern seas, she was already establishing herself in the former preserves of the Dutch East India Company; and not only to India but to South Africa, Australia, China and the islands of the Pacific, re-equipped commercial routes supported by new industrial techniques and more efficient sailing ships were beginning to fan out from the British centre. 'The ships of the English swarm like flies',

[1] See J. B. Condliffe, *The Commerce of Nations* (London, 1951), p. 203; and W. W. Rostow, *The British Economy of the Nineteenth Century* (Oxford, 1949), pp. 17-18.

[2] W. S. Jevons, *The Coal Question* (3rd ed. revised; edited by A. W. Flux (London, 1906)), p. 411.

[3] See R. A. Humphreys, *Liberation in South America, 1806-1827: The Career of James Paroissien* (London, 1952), pp. 48-9; G. S. Graham and R. A. Humphreys, *The Navy and South America, 1807-1823* (Navy Records Society, vol. CIV (London, 1962)), pp. xxiv-xxvii.

7-2

exclaimed the Pasha in Kinglake's *Eothen*; 'their printed cali-
coes cover the whole earth, and by the side of their swords
the blades of Damascus are blades of grass. All India is but
an item in the Ledger-books of the Merchants, whose lumber
rooms are filled with ancient thrones.'[1]

Birmingham, like Manchester, was to symbolize the new
industrial England, whose tentacles were spreading over the
earth. As a patriotic Brummagem wrote: 'The Arab sheik
eats his pilaf with a spoon from Birmingham. The Egyptian
pasha takes his cup of sherbet on a Birmingham waiter, lights
his harem with candelabra and crystals from Birmingham,
and nails to the wooden partitions of his yacht knick-knacks
from Birmingham on mashy paper also from Birmingham.
To feed and defend himself the Redskin uses a gun from
Birmingham, the luxurious Hindu order plate and lamps for
table and drawing-room. To the plains of South America,
for the swift-riding horsemen, Birmingham despatches spurs,
stirrup-leathers, and burnished buttons; to the Colonies, for
native planters, hatchets for cutting sugar cane, vats and
presses. The musing German needs a Birmingham strike-a-
light for his eternal pipe, and the emigrant cooks his humble
repast in a Birmingham sauce-pan on a stove from Birmingham; the name of a Birmingham manufacturer is even graven
on the tin boxes which conserve his luxuries....'[2]

All this is not to suggest that the period prior to 1815 was
devoid of far-flung commercial connections. For three centuries following the discovery of America and the Cape of
Good Hope, explorers, fishermen, traders and merchants
carried the flag far beyond the outskirts of Europe and the West

---

[1] Cabinet Edition (London, 1891), p. 13.
[2] Quoted in V. Bérard, *L'Angleterre et l'Impérialisme* (Paris, 1900), pp. 74–5.

Indies. By the close of the eighteenth century, British routes had been traced not only to the African coasts and Baltic, but to the South Atlantic and South Pacific, to the Indian Ocean and China.

In the first volume of his valuable synthesis on British expansion—*The Founding of the Second British Empire, 1763–1793,* Professor Harlow tended, I think, to exaggerate this 'swing to the East'.[1] The lines were no doubt traced by enterprising pioneer navigators, but they remained traces not trade routes. The Pacific Ocean, for example, was becoming increasingly familiar to the explorer, the whaler and the sealer, but vast reaches and innumerable islands remained untouched for decades at a time. Voyages to the Pacific were ordinarily the result of sporadic individual enterprise; men went once and might never go again. As for the Indian Ocean, compared to Europe the trade with south-east Asia was inconsiderable; because there was no large demand for European goods in any eastern country, the Indian trade was essentially a one-way traffic.[2] The trade with Africa was insignificant. The regular routes—the main network—still lay across the North Atlantic, the Channel and the Mediterranean.[3] Not

[1] Vol. 1 (London, 1952), pp. 62 ff.; see also, Peter Marshall, 'The First and Second British Empires: A Question of Demarcation', *History*, XLIX, no. 165 (February 1964), 13–18.

[2] Neither Parliament nor public devoted much time to Eastern business; indeed, after a brief discussion in 1813, Parliament dismissed Indian affairs for another twenty years. See C. H. Philips, *East India Company*, p. 299; K. M. Panikkar, *Asia and Western Dominance* (London, 1953), p. 67; Amales Tripathi, *Trade and Finance in the Bengal Presidency, 1793–1833* (Bombay, 1956), p. 305; and A. D. Gayer, W. W. Rostow and A. J. Schwartz, *The Growth and Fluctuation of the British Economy* (Oxford, 1953), p. 149.

[3] Compared with the gradually expanding overseas trade, especially to the United States, the percentage of British imports and exports to the Continent showed a decline after 1783, but the reduction was relative not absolute. See T. S. Ashton, *An Economic History of England: the 18th Century* (London, 1956), p. 154.

until the second quarter of the nineteenth century did China, India, Australia and, much later, south and west Africa, provide fields of substantial economic exploitation, and the Pacific Ocean become a profitable area of operations for the sailing tramp.

Had there been no long war, overseas trade might have shown considerable progress after 1815. As it happened, there was a period of slow transition. Deflation and poverty, governmental restrictions, and lack of markets, home and foreign, retarded the advance for about twenty years. Only in the thirties did the centre of gravity begin to shift eastward, from the North Atlantic and especially European waters, to the Indian Ocean, the China Sea and also to regions of the South Pacific.[1] By that time the merchants of Liverpool and London were as much at home in those seas as their rivals, so often their predecessors, from New York, Boston and Salem.[2]

Coal contributed enormously to the initial expansion. Because the vital factor in the profitable and economical use of a trade route was the balance between outward and return cargoes, its contribution as an export was unique. After 1815,

---

[1] From 1819 to 1834 the declared value of exports fluctuated between 35·2 and 41·6 millions, rising, however, to some 60 millions by 1845, and reaching the immense total of 190 millions by 1869. In terms of tonnage—namely, the quantity of goods transported—the growth was even more spectacular. By 1834, with the gradual reduction of shipping costs, the volume of exports had doubled over that of 1819; by 1845 it had almost quadrupled, and by 1869 it was more than ten times the 1819 figure. See A. H. Imlah, *Economic Elements in the Pax Britannica—Studies in British Foreign Trade in the Nineteenth Century* (Cambridge, Mass., 1958), pp. 94–5 and 173.

[2] There was only a slight difference in mileage from either London or New York to ports on the west coast of America. From London around the Horn to Peru was about 10,000 miles; from New York it was only some 330 miles less (A. W. Kirkaldy and A. D. Evans, *The History and Economics of Transport* (London, 1915), pp. 286–7).

when coal began to be mined on a large scale in Britain,[1] it was shipped overseas in increasing quantities as ballast. Without such a cargo to defray part or all of the outgoing expenses, import commodities such as grain, ore, cotton or lumber would have to pay for the outward voyage in ballast, as well as the return trip. Ballast coal meant lower outgoing freight rates and cheaper return cargoes of bulk commodities, and enabled Britain to extend the lead over her nearest rival, Holland, as an oceanic carrier.[2]

Laden with coal, British 'tramp' carriers could make single direct voyages to Chile for nitrates, to Argentina for hides, or to isolated Pacific Islands for guano, sandal wood and bêche-de-mer.[3] In the eighteenth century no owner or merchant would have sent a vessel so far to collect such non-luxuries as hides or guano. Saleable ballast-coal made these long journeys possible; and the other significant fact is that by the 1830's they were undertaken as a normal thing. In the ten years 1831–41, British coal exports were more than quadrupled, reaching a total of $1\frac{1}{2}$ million tons, and were more than doubled between 1841 and 1851.[4]

---

[1] Possibly around $6\frac{1}{4}$ million tons had been mined in 1780; by 1816 the total was about 16 million. See J. H. Clapham, *An Economic History of Modern Britain*, I, *1820–1850* (Cambridge, 1926), p. 431.

[2] Tonnage records of all shipping entered and cleared provide the best measurements of total British trade. See A. H. Imlah, *Economic Elements in the Pax Britannica*, pp. 172–3.

[3] Between 1838 and 1841 British trade to the Sandwich Islands was said to have increased from $20,000 to $150,000. See report of Captain Jenkin Jones, 6 November 1841, in H. U. Addington (F.O.) to Sidney Herbert (Admiralty), 4 October 1842; Ad. 1/5525. The search for guano alone extended Admiralty knowledge of the Pacific area, and often led to more accurate identification of loosely plotted islands.

[4] Ballast coal paid export duty of 7s. 6d. a ton in 1821, when 171,000 tons were shipped, and 4s. in 1831; but this duty was removed in 1834 for countries with which Britain had arranged reciprocity agreements. The duty was restored in 1842

Now the beginnings of this vast commercial expansion took place during a unique period of peace, 'a peculiar interlude in the history of civilization'.[1] 'Never in the history of Western civilization had so large a proportion of the Europeans, both in Europe and overseas, lived with so little fighting over long stretches of time, as from 1815 to 1854....'[2] Following immediately upon a general war that had continued with minor interruptions for twenty-two years, there followed a period of peace, unbroken among the chief imperial powers for almost forty years. Despite numerous internal revolutionary upsurges that threatened and sometimes occasioned outside intervention, international peace was maintained substantially intact.

In the eighteenth century when the field of competition was by later standards comparatively limited, rivalry for colonial trade and territories had precipitated and nourished almost continuous warfare. Up to the middle of the nineteenth century, when India, China, the East Indies, Latin America and Australia were becoming increasingly import-

---

at a reduced rate and repealed in 1845 for shipments in British ships. In 1850 it was repealed entirely. See W. S. Jevons, *The Coal Question* (1906 ed.), p. 313; (1865 ed.), pp. 248–9.

[1] 'There was...during the middle years of the century a peculiar interlude in the history of civilization, when all the important trading countries, except the United States, were reducing trade barriers, when all the important trading countries, again except the United States, had committed themselves to the policy and the practice of equality of treatment of all foreign countries, and when the two most important colonial powers were on their own initiative establishing the open-door in their colonial territories' (Jacob Viner, 'Peace as an Economic Problem', in *International Economics*, Glencoe, Illinois, 1951, p. 253).

[2] John U. Nef, *War and Human Progress* (Cambridge, Mass., 1950), pp. 357–8. Nef also, and I think illogically, includes in his stretches of 'unique peace' the period between 1871 and 1914, when there were many wars and preparations for war—an entirely different interlude from the former. Indeed, he emphasizes the extent to which industrial progress in the earlier nineteenth century prepared the ground for a new species of total war during those years (p. 358).

ant as export markets and sources of supply, and when new bases and territories were acquired, especially in eastern waters,[1] not only was there no warfare between the great maritime powers, there was generally an absence of that bitter politically directed competition for markets which had been so conducive to war.

To take one example—in a less tranquil age, it is highly probable that France, or some other European power, would have staked a claim or settled a colony on the almost empty continent of Australia. Had France, let us say, in the later twenties or the thirties persisted beyond the stage of casual gestures, almost certainly Britain would not have risked a war to keep her out. The leisurely colonizing activities of Britain after 1815 do not suggest that she was prepared to fight for the exclusive possession of a distant and comparatively unknown continent. On the other hand, it is equally obvious that France was not anxious to challenge with arms the leading sea power whose most pretentious claims across the oceans seemed beyond assail. Without competition, Australia became a British possession.[2] In the nineteenth century, as a consequence of one nation's overwhelming naval supremacy such phrases as 'the struggle for command of the sea' had lost all meaning.

Yet during this curious interlude, the prestige of the Royal Navy in the country and in political circles remained low, and its development as a fighting service was severely circum-

[1] British dominion in India and elsewhere continued to grow: Singapore, 1819; Assam, 1826; Falkland Islands, 1832 (1843 administered as a Crown Colony); Aden, 1839; Hong Kong, 1841; Sarawak, 1842; Sind, 1843; Punjab, 1849; Burma, 1852.

[2] See Ernest Scott, *Terre Napoléon: A History of French Explorations and Projects in Australia* (London, 1910), pp. 266–8.

scribed financially—conditions which have often led to the assumption that the power factor was ignored in the age of *Pax Britannica*, and that opulence in terms of empire was actually a matter of greater consideration by government than defence. It has, indeed, been suggested that this peculiar interlude reflected a popular *zeitgeist* as subtle in its compulsions as the bellicose expansionist creed of the 1890's, or the pacifism of the 1920's.

Judging by Commons Debates, hair-splitting taxation economies were far more exciting, and far more likely to become major political issues than problems of imperial defence.[1] Occasionally, the economy clamours struck sparks from some of the old admirals, who had retained from the Napoleonic wars an almost instinctive consciousness of the meaning of sea power in relation to empire. But, after they had passed away, there were few in parliament, or out, to preserve the tradition and teach the lessons of experience. There was 'scarcely an officer now fit for service', wrote Vice-Admiral Bowles in 1852, 'who has ever commanded a squadron at sea, and the whole of our rising generation are (without any fault of their own) perfectly inexperienced in the manœuvres of a fleet'.[2] 'So far from bringing their professional and practical experience to bear upon the real requirements of the navy and the duties that would devolve upon it in time of war', wrote John Henry Briggs, who served the Admiralty for forty-four years, 'it was with the greatest difficulty they could be prevailed upon to entertain the sub-

[1] Between 1840 and 1852 some 1150 men (excluding deserters) annually quitted the navy; in 1848 over 6000 were discharged (Roy Taylor, *Manning the Royal Navy: The Reform of the Recruiting System 1847–1861* (M.A. Thesis, 1954, University of London, p. 10)).

[2] *Thoughts on National Defence* (3rd ed., London, 1852), p. xii.

ject at all, much less regard it from its various aspects and have it thoroughly thought out....'[1] In the old days knowledge and experience had been handed down from one commander to another, but during the long and tranquil period after 1815 the tradition as well as the doctrines had faded. Indeed, only in the latter quarter of the century did naval officers like Admiral Philip Colomb begin to study history and ponder its lessons,[2] and to revive what, at its most effective, is a national art, and not the mere consequence of instinct, geography or economic compulsion.

There was substance in the nostalgic rhetoric of Blackwood's *Edinburgh Magazine* (1836): 'We see a navy, once the terror and glory of the world, silently melting away under the wish to buy good articles cheap; and our army, which once struck down Napoleon, suffered to dwindle into insignificance lest its numbers should excite the discontent of the tradesmen in our manufacturing towns.'[3] When Sir Henry Parnell urged in 1830 the abandonment at 'one fell swoop' of the Ionian Islands, Ceylon, the Cape, Mauritius and the

[1] *Naval Administrations 1827 to 1892: The Experience of 65 years* (ed. by Lady Briggs (London, 1897)), p. 295. John Henry Briggs was the son of Sir John Thomas, who had served as commissioner and accountant-general of the Victualling Board, before becoming Accountant-General of the Navy in 1832. John Henry was born in 1808, and acted as Reader to the Board of Admiralty for twenty-five years. He was knighted in 1870, on retirement from the post of chief clerk, which office he had held during the previous five years. He died in 1897.

[2] Vice-Admiral Colomb entered the navy in 1846, and was promoted captain in 1870. His penetrating writings on naval strategy cut though confused theories of local defence, and re-asserted sound doctrines of 'command', on which Mahan was to base his most influential work. Colomb was the author of *Memoirs of Admiral the Rt. Hon. Sir Astley Cooper Key* (London, 1898), the most useful study of the Royal Navy and its problems to be written during the nineteenth century. Much of his own experience is contained in *Slave Catching in the Indian Ocean* published in 1873.

[3] June 1836, p. 792.

North American provinces, the *Quarterly Review* observed with equal bitterness that 'If certain economists have their way, although history may record our glories in war, she will describe us as having sunk into a nation of pettifogging shop-keepers during the period of peace which followed these exertions.'[1] Until Palmerston began to 'cry panic' during the debates of 1844-5, and until the Duke of Wellington initiated his own naval war scare of 1847 with the pronounce-ment that steam had bridged the English Channel, the state of the Royal Navy was not a vital parliamentary issue.[2]

As a matter of fact, in the opinion of many 'reformers' inside and outside government, retrenchment in military expenditure could be regarded as a positive preparation for war, in the sense that national finances would be safeguarded from the destructive effects of a heavy burden of long-term debt. The safety and glory of the country in time of war, according to the Select Committee of Inquiry on Finance which reported in 1818, was not alone dependent on 'ships and stores and military arrangements'. '...finances recruited during peace, and wealth and industry generally diffused through the nation by all practical savings of expense and consequent diminution of burdens' were at least of equal importance.[3] 'A moderate preparation,' wrote a contemp-orary economist, 'strictly proportioned to the occasion, and

---

[1] *Quarterly Review*, XLII (1830), 520.

[2] 'Last Year', wrote Lord Auckland, the First Lord, to Lord John Russell, in 1848, 'the cry was for 20 sail of the line in the Channel, now it seems doubtful if one is not thought too many' ((30 August 1848); Russell Papers (P.R.O. series 30, vol. 22, no. 7)). The Navy Estimates, which had risen to £8,068,985 in 1847, dropped again to £6,543,255 by 1855. See also C. J. Bartlett, *Great Britain and Sea Power, 1815-1853* (Oxford, 1963), pp. 254-5.

[3] Seventh Report from the Select Committee on Finance, p. 69 (*Parl. Papers* (1818), vol. III).

not allowed to go beyond it, will save more evil than it risks; all beyond this infallibly produces more evil than it prevents; it impoverishes the nation, and renders it more easily injured by a powerful enemy, than if it had been allowed to save expense and gather strength in time of peace.'[1]

Almost inevitably then, the period of the thirties and early forties witnessed continuous reductions of the British naval force. Reconciled to being the principal object of governmental economies, and already confused by technological revolutions, which were shortly to make the old line-of-battle ships obsolete, even the Admiralty bowed before the slogans of the economists. Commerce, not ships, they were told, was the safeguard of peace, and therefore of security. Why waste money on high 'wooden walls'?

In practice, retrenchment in naval expenditure was easily applied, and without any indirect complications or political embarrassments. No other government department was so readily amenable to paring and axeing, because naval expenditure in time of peace was chiefly concerned with the purchase and preparation of materials for future exigencies.[2] Apart from reducing the numbers of seamen or putting officers on half-pay considerable reductions could be affected by paying off ships, discharging workmen and stopping the purchase of stores.[3] And such economies could be and were practised during the first half of the nineteenth century, because there was no enduring military or commercial competition.

The war-time strength of the fleet—230 ships in 1814 (in-

[1] Sir Henry Parnell, *On Financial Reform* (4th ed., 1832), p. 220.
[2] See Special Committee on Finance, 6th Report (*Parl. Papers*, 1817, vol. IV).
[3] P. H. Colomb, *Memoirs of Admiral the Rt. Hon. Sir Astley Cooper Key*, p. 429; see also C. J. Bartlett, *Great Britain and Sea Power, 1815–1853*, p. 51.

cluding frigates)—was reduced to 49 in 1820, and stood at 54 in 1838. In 1814 99 ships of the line were in commission; by 1838 only 23.[1] Between 1815 and 1840 naval estimates were reduced by almost half. In 1816 they were £9·5 million; in 1817 they went down to £6·0 million. Sir James Graham, the First Lord of the Admiralty, worked hard to cut the costs still further, and he succeeded in paring them from £5·3 million in 1830 to £4·5 in 1834, but they were up again to £5·5 million in 1840. By that time, however, the navy was absorbing only about 11 per cent of British expenditure.

In other words, power was sacrificed during this 'peaceful interlude'; but that is not the same thing as surrendering it. Although the leading exponent of progress through peace, Britain had not gone 'pacifist' under the influence of free trade. In a nutshell, the policy of sacrifice, if such it may be called, was one of defending the British empire at the least cost; and the expenses of imperial administration could most conveniently, profitably and even safely, be reduced by checking naval expenditure.

I say *safely* because, despite all the economies, the margin of security was far greater during the first half than at the end of the century, when the rise of strong naval powers outside as well as in Europe began to threaten the two-power standard of Britain. Despite the 'penny-pinching' of Cabinets and the resulting reductions in armed strength, it was possible to maintain naval supremacy on the cheap. The sword of British naval power could still be an instrument of compulsion as well as prestige, although it was rarely withdrawn more than half-way from the scabbard. A preponderant weight of sea power was still concentrated in British hands, and its possession not

[1] Graham, *Empire of the North Atlantic* (2nd ed., London, 1958), p. 266.

only guaranteed the security of trade routes anywhere on the high seas, it provided an ever-ready instrument of diplomatic pressure that might be exercised, as in Latin America, China, or in the Mediterranean, not necessarily silently, but with a minimum of international fuss and bloodshed.

To maintain the Open Door in its fullest sense meant 'power in evidence': not simply asserted thinly over trade routes, or localized in special areas like China. Even the pacific Aberdeen saw the need for such 'naval pomp and parade'. 'They have felt our power,' he wrote in September 1844, 'and they must continue to see that we are superior to other Nations if we mean to retain that ascendancy we have obtained in China.'[1] This philosophy of persuasion was fully understood by the merchants of Britain. 'How few...really understand the full meaning of Free Trade principles', exclaimed Cobden sadly in 1857. 'The manufacturers of Yorkshire and Lancashire look upon India and China as a field of enterprise which can only be kept open by force.'[2]

There is, therefore, no need to over-idealize the motives behind what became known as the *Pax Britannica*.[3] Whatever

[1] W. G. Beasley, *Great Britain and the Opening of Japan, 1834–58* (London, 1951), p. 48. Sir James Graham was reluctant to use force as a fillip to commercial expansion. None the less, as First Lord he wrote in 1834 to the Governor-General of India: 'Considering the present state of affairs in the East, I thought it better to send you a Vice-Admiral in a line-of-battle ship; so that the full impression might be produced, both as regards the importance which we attach to our relations with China, and our fixed determination to uphold the predominance of our power, which is so founded on opinion in your Eastern regions' (C. S. Parker, *Life and Letters of Sir James Graham, Second Baronet of Netherby, P.C., G.C.B. 1792–1861*, 2 vols. (London, 1907), I, 150; quoted Bartlett, *Great Britain and Sea Power*, p. 99).

[2] Quoted in William D. Grampp, *The Manchester School of Economics* (Stanford, 1960), p. 102.

[3] This description of an era following the Napoleonic wars was originally provided by Joseph Chamberlain in 1893 to illustrate the beneficent results of British rule in India.

the economies and 'penny-pinching' Britain did *not* entrust to other powers the task of ensuring the safety of her overseas communications; nor did Britain any more than did Cobden in later years count on the philosophy of free trade as the eliminator of war.[1] Even that 'economical monomaniac' Joseph Hume reluctantly confessed in Parliament that 'it was of vital importance to have an efficient navy', and he urged his countrymen to preserve Britain's supremacy at sea.[2] Other nations might enjoy the use of sea lanes, and profit by the suppression of pirates in the Persian Gulf, or the 'open door' in China. Such benefits were shared; inequalities of natural resources were ironed out by Free Trade. Yet benevolent supervision was readily transmutable into positive domination in the event of an emergency. Command of the seas, as Admiral Mahan so often remarked, was an exclusive thing; it could not be shared, and was only applicable to one nation at a time.

What were the theoretical foundations of this *de facto* monopoly of sea power? Did any of the accepted eighteenth-century doctrines of power remain to sustain the monopoly which was to be symbolized by *Pax Britannica*?

In 1815, and almost a century thereafter, British sea power owed its potency to the pursuit of no doctrine or theory; it was a fact of life resulting from the French wars. Admittedly, the association of colonies and commerce contributed, in the eighteenth century, both directly and indirectly to the growth of British sea power. Colonies, commerce and sea power had been interlinking elements; each was related to the other, and the concept of the 'three interlinking rings' as Mahan phrased

[1] See Cobden letter of 1863, quoted in John Morley, *The Life of Richard Cobden* (London, 1903), pp. 945–6.

[2] *Hansard*, new series, v, col. 1387.

it, came to be accepted as an act of faith, because British sea power had been for so long tied up with the monopoly control of colonial carrying trade. Even during war, when overseas commerce was likely to be interrupted, colonies often acquired a special value because of their strategic importance as depots and bases for the assembly, victualling and equipping of naval forces.

It would be fallacious, however, to argue that any dogma about the union of commerce, colonies and sea power had serious foundations in the nineteenth century. Until at least the middle of the century, the 'three rings' of the classical period of sea power were still linked in the minds of many men, but the evidence to support the traditional concept is lacking. As early as 1792 or thereabouts, colonial trade had ceased to be the main element in total overseas trade; the trade with Europe, including the Mediterranean, was far ahead of the total colonial trade, even when India is included as a colony. And with the beginnings of the factory age in the new century it is more than doubtful if the returns from colonial trade kept pace with the fruits of domestic industry and commerce, namely the returns from increasing internal taxation.

Nor can it be said that the colonies seriously supported British sea power in the nineteenth century in terms of men and strategic raw materials. The Newfoundland fisheries continued to be eulogized as a 'nursery for seamen', but the bulk of naval recruits came from the British Isles—from the colliers,[1] the fishing and coastal craft. Moreover, ships of war were built almost entirely in British shipyards; and although the colonies made a considerable contribution to merchant shipping, the tonnage (as well as the number of seamen) en-

[1] See Jevons, *The Coal Question* (1906 ed.), pp. 309–10; (1865 ed.), pp. 244–5.

gaged in Channel and coastal commerce was far greater than that in the colonial trade. Despite the Canadian timber preferences lasting from 1809 to 1849 the best ships' timber and masts—probably two-fifths of the total import—came from the Baltic; and, despite costly effort in the colonies, naval stores still came from the same source.

Indeed, the loss of the American colonies, it was generally assumed, had only served to increase trade with the United States—an unprovable conclusion in view of defective statistics, but one that was to be steadily propagated as the nineteenth century progressed. Nothing could be a greater mistake, wrote John R. McCulloch in 1837, 'than to suppose, as many have done, that we are mainly indebted for our wealth and the high place we occupy among the nations of the earth, to our colonial possessions. ...The truth is that we have derived ten times more advantage from our intercourse with the United States since they achieved their independence than we derived from them while we had a governor in every state, or than we have derived from all our colonies put together. And this advantage has not been accomplished by any drawbacks. We have not been obliged to purchase the timber and other commodities of the United States when we might supply ourselves better elsewhere, and we have not been obliged to keep up armaments for their protection or to encumber ourselves with the government of extensive countries on the other side of the Atlantic.'[1]

[1] *Statistical Account of the British Empire* (1839), II, 514. Many German economic historians, according to J. B. Condliffe, 'have maintained, largely on the basis of the colonial adventures in the eighteenth century, that British economic progress was based primarily upon the exploitation of colonial markets. It is significant, however, that the increase in British exports to the United States in the first half of the nineteenth century was greater than the increase to Asia' (*Commerce of Nations*, p. 208).

Similarly, it can be argued that in a period before the Dutch East Indies had become a major commercial element in the prosperity of the Netherlands, Dutch commerce throve not on colonial wealth but on relentless activity in the Baltic, Atlantic and Mediterranean. Until the outbreak of war with France, Amsterdam, the financial headquarters of Europe, had invested heavily in shipping and in the large-scale financing of enterprises engaged in international trade. Until the country was overrun by French armies in 1795, the Netherlands was once again bidding for pre-eminence as a maritime trading nation, a threat which many English merchants fully appreciated. Admittedly, Dutch trade was on sufferance during war, but in time of peace success was based not on colonies but on professional competence. The Dutch were not merely 'carriers', but large-scale merchants, manufacturers and bankers, and, like the Americans after 1783, they gave British merchants very stiff competition outside the routes and markets protected by the Navigation Acts. In other words, the prosperity of the Netherlands was not based on any effective union of colonies, trade and sea power—and neither, one might add, was that of France—and after 1815 it is impossible to find support for that fashionable dogma in the maritime history of Great Britain.

The concept of colonies supporting trade and sea power possessed historical reality only in the sense that the efficiency of the navy (in terms of seamanship and man power) did depend considerably on the size of the mercantile marine, and this again on the extent of overseas trade. After 1815, however, it may be questioned whether the British colonial carrying trade was a branch of commerce worthy of cultivation as a 'nursery'. If there had been no iron and coal and no enormous and growing industrial production, an exclusive colonial trade and fisheries might have been justified in terms of defence needs; but by the 1830's, as we have seen earlier, the channels of British foreign trade were beginning to extend themselves over the globe; and, as they settled into well-defined grooves, the total of colonial trade no longer bore any substantial proportion to the general overseas total, especially when considered against the costs of colonial administration and maintenance.[1]

By that time only two of Mahan's original three interlinking rings remained; trade and sea power; and their union was established and secure. No developments during the nineteenth century served to undermine the doctrine that national power and prosperity depended upon industry and overseas commerce, which involved in turn the upkeep of combined commercial and naval bases. And with the development of steam in the thirties, colonial bases along the main trade routes doubled in strategic importance. Such bases served not only as depots for coaling, watering, victualling and repair, but as entrepôts and centres of influence for expanding British commerce.[2]

---

[1] Estimates of expenses on account of dependencies naturally vary considerably. McCulloch was certain that the cost of colonial upkeep during the years 1833–4 was about £2,364,309 (*Statistical Account of the British Empire* (1839), II, 514). Other estimates of annual expenditure went as high as eight millions. But it is impossible to know exactly what colonies cost, because apart from the difficulty of determining what share of expenditure on army, navy and general administration should be attributed to the colonies, these items were not separated in the budget. See K. Knorr, *British Colonial Theories, 1570–1850* (Toronto, 1944; 2nd ed., London, 1963), pp. 351–2.

[2] With the exception of India, where the eighteenth-century process of expansion in self-defence continued, Britain preferred to exercise influence through the Open Door. Not until the later nineteenth century did she begin to penetrate and sometimes assimilate neighbouring hinterlands in order to safeguard existing commercial establishments on the coasts.

To Palmerston, this form of imperial acquisitiveness was the *sine qua non* of successful international trade. He believed that the British government had an unavoidable duty to the world—to keep order by extending national power and influence in advance of commerce. On 6 August 1839, in the course of a debate on Turkey, he declared his faith 'in materially supporting the commerce of Great Britain by maintaining peace; because without that, it is vain to hope for a prosperous commerce; and not only must that peace be maintained for England, but also for other countries'.[1] In sustaining this combined role of umpire and player, the Royal Navy remained an indispensable instrument of his strategic and political planning.

Less than a year after Admiral Stopford had brought Mehemet Ali to terms on the Syrian coast in November 1840, Palmerston stressed the commercial consequences of paramount sea power: 'The rivalship of European manufacturers is fast excluding our productions from the markets of Europe, and we must unremittingly endeavour to find in other parts of the world new vents for the produce of our industry. The world is large enough and the wants of the human race ample enough to afford a demand for all we can manufacture; but it is the business of the Government to open and secure the roads for the merchant.

'Will the navigation of the Indus turn out to be as great a help as was expected for our commerce? If it does, and if we succeed in our China expedition, Abyssinia, Arabia, the countries on the Indus and the new markets in China, will at no distant period give a most important extension to the range of our foreign commerce, and though in regard to the quick-

---

[1] G. H. Francis, *Opinions and Policy of Lord Palmerston* (London, 1852), p. 413.

ness of the returns, markets nearer home might be better, yet on a political point of view it must be remembered that these distant transactions not only employ our manufacturers but form our sailors.'[1]

In other words, Britain's world-wide commercial connections allowing access to most of the world's markets, and raw materials were generally unbreakable because of her supremacy at sea. During the greater part of the nineteenth century Britain was able without excessive financial effort to keep a navy numerically equal, on average, to the combined fleets of the world. Hence, in proclaiming the 'freedom of the seas', British statesmen were endangering neither commerce nor national security. The pacific British approach to international trade went hand in hand with the steady and powerful expansion of a world-encircling network of islands and bases, coaling stations and dockyards. 'Freedom of the seas' could become a British doctrine because it was based on a two-hemisphere supremacy. If, during this period, there was more talk about wealth, and less about power, it was simply owing to the fact that Britain felt confident in the possession of all the power she might on occasion feel called upon to use.[2] The purposes both of offence and defence could be fulfilled in the exercise of one instrument—a preponderant navy.

Admittedly, the achievement of what became known as the *Pax Britannica* was by no means the simple consequence of naval power wielded with sensible restraint by the self-appointed policemen of the world. It was the result of varied

[1] C. K. Webster, *The Foreign Policy of Palmerston, 1830–41*, 2 vols. (London, 1951), II, 750–1.
[2] See Jacob Viner's review of Eli Heckscher, *Mercantilism* in *Economic History Review*, VI (1945–6), 99–101.

forces and circumstances, the chief of which was Britain's industrial supremacy, which made possible a phenomenal commercial development. The fact that the great market of the United Kingdom together with the wider markets of an enormous empire was steadily opening to the products of other states not only stimulated general economic activity, it contributed to relax international tensions within the whole trading world. If maritime power were unattainable for rival nations, this was not true of wealth; and the growth of free trade, which introduced a kind of international equality in the sharing of economic benefits, encouraged acquiescence in the British hegemony.

Indeed, it was this general desire to avoid war that made the so-called age of *Pax Britannica* possible. It is true that men-of-war were used on occasion to effect specific ends whether in Greece, Latin America or China, but it would be wrong to suggest that the Royal Navy imposed a British peace on the world. There was, for example, no effort to stop the French from entering Algiers in 1830, or Mexico in 1863 or Indo-China in the sixties, nor to keep the Americans out of Japan in the fifties, or the North from blockading the South during the American Civil War. Britain was in no position to seek or to ensure the peace of mankind by means of her fleet. 'We cannot afford to be the Knight Errant of the World', Lord Rosebery told Queen Victoria, 'careering about to redress grievances and help the weak.'[1] On the other hand, the general quiescence of European powers gave Britain the opportunity to use her navy not only as a means of conducting anything from a demonstration to a local war, but as an effective restraining force in the interests of a Euro-

---

[1] Crewe, *Lord Rosebery*, II, 426.

pean balance. The result was, on the whole, a political stabilization which suggested to more optimistic 'Free Traders' the possibility of continuous material progress by peaceful process.

After the middle of the nineteenth century, British ascendancy in the fields of industry, finance, commerce and shipping was complete. No other power had sufficiently developed its industrial resources to offer serious competition. The iron, coal and other basic materials required for military production were available within the British Isles, and British manpower was sufficient to exploit them. In terms of a 'war economy' she was self-sufficient. The shift from timber to iron in ship construction, the introduction of armour plate and the shell-firing rifled gun gave an enormous advantage to the country possessing the most advanced metallurgical mills and capable of the largest production of pig iron.[1] Similarly, during the course of evolution from sail to steam, the possession of vast coalfields and well distributed coaling-stations confirmed the pre-eminence which had been acquired in two centuries of commercial and territorial expansion under sail.

Master of all she surveyed, Britain was, therefore, in a unique position to scrap traditional doctrines of national advantage, and to influence by example the trend towards free trade. Because her imperial security was rarely threatened after 1805 there was no need for any ostentatious assertion of maritime rights. Economic predominance was simply not compatible with military weakness; and because no jealous disputants were capable of challenging her maritime monopoly, British policies of economic co-operation in terms of

[1] See William E. Livezey, 'Sea Power in a Changing World', *Marine Corps Gazette*, U.S.A. (May 1949), part II.

free trade, peace and prosperity, were generally acceptable. The established superiority of the Royal Navy discouraged competition.

Obviously, however, this acceptance of the British way of international life was possible only so long as other countries were willing to accept dependence, at least in the overseas colonial world, on the philosophy and will of another power, and were not actively determined to reduce or eliminate the special advantages which that power derived from her naval supremacy. When European states began to re-examine their national policies in the light of their prospective industrialization and when they started to build their own steam machinery, enlarge and re-equip their own factories, lay down iron rails, and construct iron hulls, the age of *Pax Britannica* was over.

The delayed impact of this revolution has obscured its fundamental importance in history. The crucial turning-point in our affairs was reached almost a hundred years ago when European nations, suddenly aware that science had upset the balance between offence and defence in favour of the weaker power, initiated their own industrial revolutions, involving not only weapons, missiles, armour, tools and tactics, but the whole organization and control of what are called strategic materials. In the eighteenth century the power of a state had often been measured in terms of such imports as bullion, sugar, spices, masts or timber; in the new age, the elements of military strength were to be found in raw materials such as coal, tin, copper, wool—and, later on, nickel, tungsten, cotton, oil and rubber—many of which were only available in distant areas overseas.

Coerced by the depression of the seventies into abandoning

free trade for protection, the major powers of Europe recognized that a key to greater self-sufficiency and strength lay in actually controlling as much productive overseas territory as they could lay hands on. W. L. Langer has described this concept as 'preclusive imperialism'—'a concomitant of the onrushing industrial revolution...so compelling that most statesmen, even the skeptical Bismarck were carried away by it'.[1] It was not British abuse of her naval supremacy, and of her almost monopolistic control of the oceans, that ultimately led other European nations to aggressive policies of overseas expansion and annexation. Such nations were guided by political considerations and impelled by their own economic growth.

In an age when science had begun to erase the heavy premium that geography, ships and seamanship had given to Great Britain, the machines of industry had opened up to all well-endowed countries new and tempting vistas of military capacity, prestige, and independence. Command of the sea was obviously beyond their reach; on the other hand, it might be pushed beyond the reach of the benevolent disposer who had for so long reigned supreme in three great oceans. Hence, without much understanding of their use, they proceeded, in the manner of Wilhelm II, to build navies to support national policies that were initially a consequence of economic compulsions accompanying industrial revolution and technological change. In other words, the search for overseas resources, with which to feed the new machinery, drove otherwise moderate governments inexorably along unknown military paths marked by accumulations of triple-expansion engines and turbines, torpedo-boats and submarines.

[1] 'Farewell to Empire', *Foreign Affairs* (October 1962), p. 120.

In the nineteenth century the British empire was not only world-wide; it was scattered, and therefore vulnerable. Yet, allowing for minor lapses, Great Britain could safely and effectively defend colonial trade and territories anywhere. During this period the Royal Navy was the chief guarantor of imperial security and continued expansion. By the end of the century, however, the principle of universal command had to be surrendered in favour of a strategy of local concentration. At the beginning of 1896 Britain stood completely isolated. France, Russia, Turkey, Germany and the United States were openly hostile, and in view of the general European situation the Admiralty were in no position to reinforce overseas stations in the event of emergency. Indeed, during the Venezuelan crisis of 1896 the narrow margin of superiority over the Dual Alliance in European waters made it impossible to send additional ships to the North American and West Indies squadron.[1] Five years later the Hay-Pauncefote treaty signalized the surrender of the British position of equality in the Caribbean. No longer able to challenge the United States in the western Atlantic, Britain had taken the first step towards conciliating a non-European naval rival. The second step— the Japanese Alliance of 1902—was simply a confirmation of the fact that she could no longer distribute her naval forces over two hemispheres and maintain the two-power standard.

Meanwhile, with growing competition for strategic war materials, the security of overseas routes became increasingly important to vulnerable European powers. The complex war

---

[1] In all probability war was never likely, but the Admiralty's failure to take even precautionary measures must have been the result of the general European situation. The Americans possessed only three first-class battleships, and one or two second-class battleships. See A. J. Marder, *British Naval Policy, 1880–1905*; published in the U.S. under the title: *The Anatomy of British Sea Power*, pp. 255–7.

economy of a nation could be immobilized as a consequence of naval blockade. The only alternative was the peace-time stockpiling of massive reserves of oil, rubber, ferro-alloys and such like, adequate to meet the output required by the new scale of competitive armaments in time of war. This precaution, curiously enough, the European nations failed to take, with the result that in two world wars command of the sea was to be of greater significance than ever before. The safe transfer of war materials, especially from North America, was vital to a favourable military balance. In 1914, and again in 1939, the survival of Great Britain was contingent upon the maintenance of maritime communications, made possible eventually by an unqualified allied naval supremacy.

It is an interesting commentary on human affairs that Mahan's exposition of the influence of sea power on the course of European and American expansion should have occurred at the very time when new instruments of the Industrial Revolution were beginning to erode principles and theories upon which his doctrines were based. Under the impact of scientific and technological advances, British command of the sea, hitherto based on a unique combination of geographical, economic and human considerations, had already begun to disintegrate.

With the coming of the aeroplane, an empire based on control of the sea was no longer possible. Battleships and cruisers were not sufficient of themselves to maintain maritime communications. Mahan's dictum had lost its validity within two decades of its pronouncement. And within the last few years, a single instrument—the nuclear warhead—has increased man's powers of destruction to a point that remains beyond his powers of self-defence.

The Illusion of 'Pax Britannica'

Today we have reached the last watershed, whence earlier periods become comprehensible in their seeming simplicity. Looking backward from the confusion of our own times—from a world racked and menaced by incurable tensions—the historian is granted a perspective not hitherto obtainable. He can now see the nineteenth century as one epoch of history, when Britain was able to use her naval supremacy to maintain a balance between conflicting European land powers to keep the peace: an age of equilibrium, that permitted, not the forceful imposition of a *Pax Britannica*, but the international acceptance of a British monopoly of the seas which Mahan rightly identified with world power.

INDEX

Aberdeen, Fourth Earl of, on uses of naval power, 111

Achin, 45

Acre, 77

Aden, 10, 36, 41, 65, 73, 86, 90; British occupation of, 74-5

Aden, Gulf of, 31

Admiralty Memorandum on Imperial Defence (1902), 8

Admiralty, Lords of: policies in the latter half of the nineteenth century, 58, 59, 60, 78; calm acceptance of southern expansion of the French Empire, 79; submission to defence economies, 109; effects of isolation on, 123

Aeroplane, effect on 'command of the sea', 28-9, 124

Afghanistan, British retreat from (1842), 88

Albuquerque, Affonso d', 54

Alexander the Great, 63

Alexandretta, 86, 92

Alexandria, 37, 64, 65, 66, 69; conventions at (1839), 77, 87, 90, 93

Algiers, 68, 119

Algoa Bay, 34

American Civil War, 119

American Revolution, see War of American Independence

Amiens, Peace of, 39

Amirante Islands, 42

Amsterdam, 36, 98, 115

Andaman Islands, 45

Anglo-Dutch Treaty of 1824, 54, 55

Ankara, 92

Anson, Admiral George, 61

Antwerp, 55, 56

Arabia, 69, 77; British oil interests in, 93, 95

Arabian coast, 70

Arabian Sea, 31, 32, 77; British control of, 89

Armada, see Spanish Armada

Atfeh, on the Nile, 66

Atlantic Ocean, 20, 25, 27, 31, 79, 101, 115; the shift of power from the Mediterranean, 64

Auckland, George Eden, First Earl of (First Lord of the Admiralty), on navy estimates (1848), 108n.

Australia, 99, 104, 105

Axelson, Professor Eric, on Covilhã's explorations, 34

Bagdad, 66, 73, 86, 87, 92, 93

Bagdadbahn, 93

Bahrein, 75

Baltic, ships' timber from, 114; Dutch activity in, 115

Bangkok, 57

Basra, 87, 88, 91, 92

Batavian Republic, 47

Bay of Bengal, 31, 32, 42, 44-6

Bay of Biscay, 23

Beirut, 87

Bencoolen, 48

Bermuda, 53

Birmingham, symbol of the new industrial England, 100

Bismarck, Prince, 91, 122

Bizerta, 79, 80

Black Sea, 67, 71, 82, 84, 89

Board of Trade and Plantations, 16, 18

Bombay, 39, 42, 45, 46, 58, 65, 66, 85, 86, 92

Borneo, 42

Boscawen, Admiral Edward, 47

Bosphorus, 67, 70-1, 73

Boston, 102

Index

Index

Index

Industrial Revolution, 27–8, 42, 98; and development of European trade, 113; and naval power, 121–2, 124

Ionian Islands, 107

Italy, 77, 81

Jacobites, 23

Japan, industrial development of, 61

Japanese Alliance (1902), 123; capture of Singapore, 62

Java, 27, 38, 56; return of, to Holland (1816), 48, 54

Joinville, Prince de, 68n., 69

Karimun Islands, 52

Kharak, 66, 88

Khurshid Pasha, 75, 77

Konieh, 71, 93

Kronstadt, 81

La Bourdonnais, Bertrand-François Mahé, Comte de (governor-general of Ile de France and Ile Bourbon 1735–46), 44, 61

Labuan Island, 42, 60

Laisser-faire, policy of, 58

Lamarche, Hyppolyte, 68

Langer, W. L., and 'preclusive imperialism', 122

Latin America, trade with, 99, 104, 119

Laughton, John Knox, paper on 'The Scientific Study of Naval History', 4; founder of the Navy Records Society, 6

Leopold, Prince of Saxe-Coburg-Gotha, 55

Lesseps, Ferdinand de, 90

Letters of marque, 56

Light, Captain Francis, 46

Lisbon, 36

Liverpool, 102

London, 36, 43, 65, 84, 98–9

Louis Philippe, King of France, 72, 73, 77

Louis XIV, the wars of, 20

Louisiana, 21

McCulloch, John R., and colonial trade, 114, 116n.

Mackesy, Piers, *The War for America, 1775-1783*, 24–5

Mackinder, Sir Halford, 10; lecture to the Royal Geographical Society (1904), 29–30

Madagascar, 32, 39, 41, 42, 57

Madeira, 38

Madras, 39, 44

Mahan, Alfred Thayer, 22, 25, 28, 63, 112, 116, 124, 125; *The Influence of Sea Power upon History*, 4

Mahmoudie Canal, 66

Malacca, 36, 48, 54

Malaya, 33, 52

Maldive Archipelago, 42

Malta, 68, 69, 76, 79, 90

Manchester, symbol of the new industrial England, 100

Mauritius, 27, 40, 41, 42, 49, 53n., 70, 107; the capture of, 46, 48

Mediterranean, 14, 20, 23, 27, 32, 34, 36, 37, 53, 101, 113, 115; corridor (chap. III), 63–95; the shift of power to the Atlantic, 64; British naval forces in, 76–7; the Black Sea outlet, 82

Mehemet Ali, 65, 69, 70, 73, 74, 82; 87, 117

Melville Island, 59

Mercantilism, theory of, 16–17

Mesopotamia, 73, 86, 89, 93

Mexico, 119

Minorca, 69

Molucca Islands, 48

Monsoons, 31–2, 35, 36, 37n., 45, 86

Moscow, 84

Moslems, and trade in the Indian Ocean, 37, 37n.

Mosul, 93

Mozambique, 36, 56

Mozambique Channel, 39

Napoleon III, 68, 81

Napoleon, campaigns to distract, 27; consequences of his Egyptian campaign, 39

Index

Royal Navy (*cont.*)
vasion, 23; War of American Independence, 25–7; deployment of the
fleet in 1839, 79n.; strength of, 80n.,
105; decline of, 106n., 108n.;
'showing the flag', 111n.; bases for,
116; as Palmerston's indispensable
instrument, 117
Russia, in the Dardenelles, 70, 71;
occupation of Constantinople, 81;
and the Treaty of Paris (1850), 81;
policy towards Persian Gulf, 85, 88;
war with Turkey (1877–8), 92, 123

Sailing techniques, 12–13; the im-
provement of, 38, 39, 109; develop-
ment of steam, 116, 120; the impact
of the Industrial Revolution on, 121,
122
St Helena, 38, 41
St Lawrence River, 11
Salem, 102
Salisbury, Earl of, 80, 84, 94
Sarawak, 60
Scurvy, 38, 38n.
Select Committee of Inquiry on
Finance (1818), 108
Senegal River, 32
Seven Years War, 20, 24, 44–5, 65
Seychelles Archipelago, 42
Seymour, Admiral Frederick B. P.,
bombards Alexandria (1882), 90
Shatt-el-Arab, 84, 88
Ships: S.S. *Hugh Lindsay*, 86
Shuvalov, Peter, 95n.
Siam, 57
Sicily, 67
Simonstown, 53n., 58
Singapore, 10, 41, 52, 54, 58, 62; the
Malta of the East, 53
Smith, Adam, 18
Sofala, 34
Spanish Armada, 12–13
Spanish Succession, War of, 18, 23
Spice Islands, 27, 33, 38
Stopford, Admiral Sir Robert, 77, 117

Strait of Bab-el-Mandeb, 10, 31
Strait of Dover, 10
Strait of Gibraltar, 10, 79
Straits of Malacca, 10, 31, 42, 48, 51,
52, 56, 69
Straits of Singapore, 54
Straits of Sunda, 38, 48
Straits Settlements, 43
Submarine, effect on 'command of the
sea', 28–9
Suez Canal, 83, 90, 91, 93, 95;
Convention of, 1888, 90n.
Suez, Isthmus of, 64–6, 69, 74, 78, 90, 94
Suffren, Pierre-André, bailli de, 44, 61
Sumatra, 31, 38, 48, 52
Syria, 69, 71, 77, 86, 91, 92

Temenggong, Data', 52
Temperley, H. W. V., and the Anglo-
Dutch Treaty (1824), 54n.
Tigris-Euphrates rivers and valley, 31,
73, 77; route, 84, 87–8
Toulon, 68; French fleet at, 78; as a
Russian repair base, 82
Treasury, 40; influence on naval
strategy, 57, 109
Treaty of Paris (1856), 81
Treaty of Tordesillas (1494), 10
Treaty of Unkiar Skelessi (8 July
1833), 71, 84, 86
Treaty of Utrecht, 19
Trincomalee, 45, 47, 58
Tripoli, 69
Tunis, 69; French occupation of, 79
Turkey, 64, 65, 93, 94n., 95n.; weakness
of, 70. 73, 82, 89; war with Russia
(1877–8), 92; parliamentary debate
on, 117

United States, British trade with, 114,
123
Utrecht, Treaty of, 19

Van Leur, J. C., 37
Van Pallandt, Baron, 41
Van Riebeeck, Jan, 38

131

Index

Printed in the United Kingdom
by Lightning Source UK Ltd.
134308UK00001B/165/P